THE FIX

A Business Fable For When Your People Aren't Broken, But Your Process Is

Betsy Kauffman

Published by Freiling Agency

www.freilingagency.com

Paperback ISBN: 978-1-969826-52-8

Hardcover ISBN: 978-1-969826-53-5

E-Book ISBN: 978-1-969826-54-2

For Mom and Dad

Thank you for the love, laughter, and a childhood that still shapes every room I walk into. I miss you every day. I hope this book makes you proud.

CONTENTS

Prologue: *A Note from Jayne*......7

Chapter One: *The Drive In*......11

Chapter Two: *The Podcast*......15

Chapter Three: *The Call*......19

Chapter Four: *Meet Meridian*......25

Chapter Five: *The Engagement Begins*......31

Chapter Six: *What They Said About Grace*......39

Chapter Seven: *What They Said About James*......45

Chapter Eight: *The Coaching Team*......51

Chapter Nine: *The Feedback Session*......57

Chapter Ten: *The Bad Meeting*......63

Chapter Eleven: *Before the Room*......67

Chapter Twelve: *Day One Morning: The Foundation*......71

Chapter Thirteen: *State of the Union*......77

Chapter Fourteen: *The Strategy Problem*......83

Chapter Fifteen: *The Crack*......87

Chapter Sixteen: *Day Two: The Hard Conversation*......93

Chapter Seventeen: *One Word*......99

Chapter Eighteen: *The Coaches Debrief*......105

Chapter Nineteen: *Contact with Reality*..........111

Chapter Twenty: *What James Sees Now*..........117

Chapter Twenty-One: *The Moment of Truth*..........123

Chapter Twenty-Two: *Jayne Reflects*..........127

Epilogue: *Six Months Later*..........131

Afterword: *A Note from the Author*..........137

PROLOGUE

A Note from Jayne

I've been doing this work for twenty years, and I can tell you almost exactly how the first call goes.

The CEO is smart. Usually self-made, or close to it. They've built something real — a company with revenue, employees, customers who depend on them. They're not calling me because things are falling apart. Things are pretty good, not great by some measure, but good enough.

They're calling me because of a person. There's always a person.

Sometimes it's the CFO who can't communicate without putting people on the defensive. Sometimes it's a VP of Sales who hits his numbers but leaves a trail of wreckage behind him. Sometimes it's a COO who's great with systems but terrible with people.

And sometimes — more often than you'd think — it's the head of HR. The person whose entire job is to understand people, developed a blind spot to herself somewhere along the way.

The CEO has usually been patient. They want me to know that. They *think* they have given good feedback. They've had conversations. They've hoped things would improve. But now they're calling me because they've decided: this person is the problem. If we can just fix him or her — or, if we can't fix them, replace them — everything else will fall into place.

I listen. I take notes. I ask a few questions.

And then, almost every time, I start to see it — the thing they can't see from where they're standing.

The person they're calling about isn't fine. They usually do need support. The feedback is usually at least partially accurate.

But they are not the problem. They are the *symptom.*

The problem lives somewhere else. It lives in the unclear strategy that shifts every quarter. In the decisions that get made and then quietly unmade. In the meetings where everyone agrees and nothing changes. In the gap between what the leader says and what the leader does.

The problem, most of the time, lives at the top.

I don't say that to indict anyone. The CEOs I work with are really good people. They care deeply about their companies and the people in them. They are not the villains of this story.

But they called me about someone else. And I've learned that means it's time to look somewhere they haven't looked yet.

This is the story of one of those calls. And what happened after I answered it.

ACT ONE: THE WRONG DIAGNOSIS

CHAPTER ONE

The Drive In

James Wilson had a ritual.

Every Monday morning, he left the house at seven-fifteen, stopped at the same coffee shop two miles from the office, ordered the same medium dark roast he'd been ordering since they opened, and drove the last eight minutes to work in silence.

The silence was intentional. His wife had suggested it years ago, back when the company was young and he was carrying it home every night in his jaw and his shoulders. *Give yourself a few minutes to just be in the car,* she'd said. *Before the day starts.*

It had worked, for a while.

Lately, the silence wasn't peaceful. It was just a container for everything he hadn't resolved yet.

This particular Monday, James was somewhere on the stretch of Route 9 between the coffee shop and the office when he became aware that he'd been replaying the same conversation in his head for three miles. The one he'd had with Grace last Thursday. The one where he'd tried — again — to give her feedback about how she was coming across in leadership team meetings, and she'd nodded along in that way she had, the way that felt like agreement but never seemed to produce any change.

He'd been having variations of that conversation for two years.

Grace Matthews had been with Meridian almost since the beginning. Employee number three, back when the company was twelve people and a shared dream. She'd grown with it — from office manager to HR generalist to, eventually, Chief Human Resources Officer — and James loved her for that. The loyalty. The institutional memory. The way she could tell you the story of almost any employee or client relationship going back fifteen years.

But Meridian wasn't twelve people anymore. It was pushing five hundred, with revenues closing in on $180 million, and the company James needed today was not the company Grace had grown up in. The leadership team had changed. The strategy had gotten more complex. The pace had accelerated.

And Grace, somewhere along the way, had stopped accelerating with it.

She was still doing the job the way she'd always done it — with warmth and history and genuine effort — but effort wasn't the same as impact. The other leaders had started coming to James quietly, with their frustrations. She wasn't getting them the talent they needed. She was slow to respond to things that felt urgent. She had a way of dominating conversations with her own perspective, unaware — or indifferent — to the effect it had on the room.

He'd tried to tell her. Multiple times.

She'd nod. She'd agree. Nothing would change.

Annual planning was seven weeks away. The planning was supposed to produce a clear strategy for the year, a set of priorities everyone owned, and a team ready to execute. The last two annual planning sessions had produced exactly none of those things. Lots of good discussion, some laughs, drinks afterwards. A slide deck that lived on a shared drive. And then Q1 would start and everyone would more or less go back to doing what they'd already been doing.

This year had to be different. He knew that. His leadership team knew that. The team knew that — or they should have.

And James couldn't walk into that room with Grace the way she was.

He turned into the parking garage and found his spot and sat there for a moment with the engine running.

He didn't want to fire her. He really didn't. But he was running out of other ideas.

He turned off the engine. Picked up his phone. Opened his podcast app, remembered he hadn't finished the one he'd started on Thursday, and hit play.

He had eight minutes before the day started. He figured he'd listen while he walked in.

CHAPTER TWO

The Podcast

The walk from the parking garage to the front door of Meridian's office was about four minutes, which was usually just enough time to shift from wherever James's head had been to wherever it needed to be.

Not today.

He had his earbuds in and was halfway across the lobby when the podcast host said something that made him slow down.

"—and I think the thing that trips up so many leaders is that they're incredibly good diagnosticians when it comes to everyone else on their team, and almost completely blind when it comes to their own role in the dynamic."

The host's guest was a woman named Jayne Swan. He hadn't heard of her. The episode had been in his queue for a few weeks, recommended by an algorithm he didn't fully trust, and he'd only started it because the title had caught his eye: *When the Problem Isn't the Problem.*

He stopped at the elevator and pressed the button.

"Can you give us an example?" the host asked.

"Sure," the woman said. She had a calm voice. Measured. Like someone who had seen enough that she no longer needed to perform urgency. "I worked with a CEO a few years back who was convinced his COO was the issue. And honestly? Some of the feedback about the

COO was real. He did have blind spots. He did need development."

"But?"

"But the reason nothing was getting done wasn't the COO's blind spots. It was that nobody in that organization — including the COO — knew what they were actually supposed to be executing *toward.* The strategy changed every time the CEO read a new book or came back from a conference. People had stopped committing to things because they'd learned, over time, that commitment didn't matter. Whatever they committed to would probably be different in six weeks anyway."

The elevator opened. James didn't get in.

"So what did you do?" the host asked.

"I started with the COO, like I was hired to. But eventually I had to have an honest conversation with the CEO. And that conversation started with one question: *What is the last decision you made that was successfully executed by your leadership team?*

"What did he say?"

She paused. "He changed the subject. Three times. And then he said he'd have to think about it."

"And that told you everything."

"That told me everything."

The elevator doors closed without him.

James stood in the lobby, alone, the morning foot traffic moving around him. He was aware that he was standing still in a way that probably looked strange. He didn't move.

What is the last decision you made that was successfully executed by your leadership team?

He ran back through the last several months. The hiring debate. The new territory expansion. The reorg conversation that had been happening, in various forms, for almost a year. In every single one of those moments, he could see himself clearly — asking for input, weighing all the perspectives, bringing people together to talk it through.

He could not see himself making a call.

He pressed the elevator button again.

By the time he reached his floor, he had already looked up Jayne Swan's website on his phone. By the time he reached his desk, he had read the About page twice. And by nine-fifteen, after his first two meetings of the morning, he had typed out a message to the contact address on her site.

He deleted it. Rewrote it. Deleted it again. Then he wrote a simpler version:

I heard you on a podcast this morning. I think you might be describing my company. Would you be open to a conversation?

He hit send before he could rewrite it again.

CHAPTER THREE

The Call

Jayne called him back the next afternoon.

He'd been in back-to-back meetings all morning and had almost forgotten he'd sent the message, which was probably why he answered more honestly than he might have if he'd had time to prepare.

She introduced herself, thanked him for reaching out, and then said: "Tell me what's going on."

So he did.

He told her about Meridian — the growth, the team, the annual planning cycle that kept producing decks instead of results. He told her about the talent gaps and the execution problems and the strategy that never seemed to fully stick. He talked for probably ten minutes without stopping, and she let him.

And then, almost without meaning to, he told her about Grace.

He was careful about it. He said *I want to be fair to her* before he started, and he meant it. He talked about her tenure and her loyalty and the things she genuinely brought to the organization. But eventually he got to the part he'd been building toward: the feedback that didn't land, the hiring that kept missing, the way she showed up in the room, the sense that the role had grown in ways she hadn't grown with it.

He finished. There was a brief silence on the line.

"Okay," Jayne said. "Tell me about Grace. And then tell me — what does the rest of your team look like *around* her?"

James opened his mouth. Closed it. "What do you mean?"

"I mean your other direct reports. Your leadership team. How are they functioning?"

"They're — good. I mean, there are always things. Olivia is our CFO, still getting up to speed — she's only been with us about eight months but she's smart and a great hire, a recommendation from a golfing buddy when Grace couldn't find any good candidates, by the way."

He paused. "Alex is our COO. He's my son."

He said it the way people say things they know will land a certain way — quickly, with a slight brace.

"He finished his MBA, went to work for someone else for a few years, and just recently came back to take on the COO role. It's a newly created position — I decided we needed it because the current Ops leader was good but not strategic enough to lead at this level. Alex has obviously grown up knowing the ins and outs of Meridian. He worked here in various capacities all through high school and college."

"And your CMO?"

"Will. Will Parks. He's been with us for ten or so years. Done a good job growing with the company. Very creative, not afraid to speak his mind." A beat. "He and Grace have a tight relationship. Maybe a bit too tight at times."

"What does execution look like on your leadership team?" Jayne asked. "Not any individual—the team itself.

When you leave a planning session, does everyone know exactly what they own and by when?"

The pause was longer this time. "We're working on that," James said.

"Of course," she said, and her tone didn't shift at all — no judgment in it, no trap. James looked at the window. Outside, the parking lot was gray and ordinary under a cloudy sky.

"That's something we're going to work on at the annual planning session ," he said.

"When is that?"

"Seven weeks."

"Good," she said. "That's actually good timing."

There was something in the way she said it — not reassuring exactly, more like someone who had just confirmed a suspicion and was already thinking about next steps. It would have bothered him from someone else. From her, it felt oddly steadying.

"Can I ask you something?" he said.

"Of course."

"Do you think Grace is the problem?"

The silence this time was shorter, but it felt more deliberate.

"I think Grace may have real development needs," Jayne said carefully. "I think some of what you've described about how she's landing with the team is worth taking seriously. I wouldn't dismiss that." A beat. "But I've been doing this long enough that when a CEO calls me about one person, I've learned to get curious about the whole system before I start drawing conclusions."

"The whole system," James repeated.

"The whole system. Which includes you."

He'd been half-expecting that. He still wasn't entirely sure how he felt about it.

"What would that look like?" he asked. "Working with you."

She walked him through it — starting with Grace, but expanding to the full leadership team, and ultimately building toward the annual planning session as a real inflection point. Not just a strategy exercise or a fun offsite . A chance to reset how the team worked together.

"I'd bring in a couple of colleagues to support the other leaders," she said. "I'd work with you directly. And before any of that, I'd want to do 360 feedback across the whole team — including you."

"Including me."

"Including you."

He didn't say anything for a moment.

"My guess is that you already have a sense of what it might say," Jayne said. Her tone was still calm. Still even. "Most leaders do, if they're honest with themselves."

James thought about standing in the lobby that morning with the elevator doors closing in front of him. He thought about the question she'd asked on the podcast — the one about the last decision he'd made that was successfully executed.

He still didn't have an answer to it.

"Okay," he said. "Let's do it."

CHAPTER FOUR

Meet Meridian

Jayne's first request, before she sat down with anyone individually, was simple.

"I'd like to observe a leadership team meeting," she told James. "Don't change anything about how you normally run it. Don't warn them to be on their best behavior. Just let me sit in the corner and watch."

James had hesitated slightly at that last part. "They're going to wonder who you are."

"Tell them I'm a consultant you've brought in to support the team's development. That's true. Just don't tell them more than that yet."

The meeting was a Tuesday at nine. Eight chairs around a long table in the conference room they called the Fishbowl — all glass walls, visible from the open office floor beyond. Jayne arrived early and took a chair along the wall, away from the table, with a notepad and a coffee and nothing else.

She had learned, years ago, that the most useful thing she could do in a first observation was to pay attention not to what people said, but to where they looked. To the unspoken behaviors and mannerisms which showed up when they were in a typical, comfortable setting.

James came in at nine-oh-two, which Jayne noted was two minutes late to his own meeting, and immediately created warmth in the room just by walking into it. That was a real gift, she thought. Some leaders had it and some didn't — the ability to make people feel, simply by arriving, that things were going to be okay.

He smiled at a few people, dropped his laptop on the table, and said "alright, let's get into it" in the tone of someone who was genuinely glad to be there.

She watched the room respond to him. Shoulders dropped slightly. Faces opened up. Whatever low-level tension had been present before he walked in quietly released itself.

She made a note.

Olivia Scott sat directly across from the door, which Jayne suspected was not an accident. She was the kind of person who liked to see the full room — to know where everyone was before the conversation started. She had a legal pad and a good pen and she used them both. She didn't say much in the first twenty minutes, but Jayne noticed she wrote something down almost every time James spoke and twice more when he didn't follow up on a question he'd just asked.

Jayne had been told Olivia was eight months in. She looked like someone in the middle of a very careful audit — not of the financials, but of the organization itself. Collecting data. Not yet sure what to do with it.

She would be useful, Jayne thought, when she trusted the room enough to say what she actually thought.

Alex Wilson sat to his father's left, which was either instinctive or deliberate, and Jayne couldn't tell which. He was younger than she'd expected from James's description — late twenties, with the kind of energy that fills a room not through volume but through a kind of contained intensity, like someone who is always slightly more prepared than the situation requires.

He had done his homework. When the group got to a discussion about a logistics bottleneck in the company's fulfillment process, Alex pulled up a document he'd clearly prepared in advance, walked through three options with their tradeoffs, and presented a recommendation with calm, clear confidence.

It was good. Genuinely good.

Jayne watched James respond. He nodded along. He said "this is great work, Alex." And then he said "what does everyone else think?" and opened the floor to the room, and Jayne watched something happen in Alex's face — almost imperceptible, there and gone — that she recognized immediately.

He'd made a recommendation. He'd expected a decision. What he'd gotten instead was a committee.

She wrote two words on her notepad: *Needs resolution.*

Will Parks arrived with an extra coffee, and placed it in front of an empty chair across from him. Jayne presumed it was for Grace, which Jayne clocked as either genuine thoughtfulness or a very practiced social habit. Probably both, she decided. He had the easy confidence of someone who had been in rooms like this for a long time and had made a quiet study of how to be comfortable in them.

He was good in the meeting. Articulate, perceptive, often the person who found the language to bridge two competing perspectives. When Alex and Grace got slightly sideways over a recruiting process that had apparently been a recurring tension, it was Will who said "I think what we're both getting at is—" and then offered a reframe that let both of them stand down without losing face.

Useful skill, Jayne thought. Also, potentially, a way of making sure nothing ever truly gets resolved.

She watched him look at James after he offered the reframe — a brief glance, checking the temperature — and she noted that too.

Grace Matthews was the last one in, arriving at nine-oh-seven with a travel mug and a three-ring binder that looked like it had been in continuous use since the early 2000s. She sat across from Will and at the far end of the table from James, which put her at the periphery of the natural eye contact loop, and Jayne wasn't sure whether Grace was aware of that or not. She picked up the coffee cup Will had placed at her empty seat and winked at him across the table. He nodded with an "of course" smirk.

She came alive when someone mentioned a client name from several years back — context that nobody else at the table had. She provided it generously, in detail, and she was right. It was valuable. The table needed it.

And then she kept talking.

Not egregiously. Not in a way that anyone would describe, if asked, as a problem. But Jayne could see the moment when the room had gotten what it needed and Grace had kept going — the almost invisible micro-adjustments of people who were politely waiting for a place to re-enter. Will looked down at his phone. Alex shifted in his seat. Olivia's pen pausing over her notepad.

James let it run. He didn't redirect. He nodded, said "that's really helpful context, Grace," and then waited for a natural pause before moving on.

Grace didn't notice any of it.

Jayne kept her face neutral and wrote a single word: *Unaware.*

Then, after a moment, she crossed it out and wrote something else:

Unprotected.

It was a small but important distinction. *Unaware* suggested something internal — a deficit in self-perception, a gap in emotional intelligence. And that might be true. But what Jayne had also seen was a leader at the head of the table who had never, as far as she could tell, given Grace a clear signal that the behavior was costing her anything. No gentle redirect. No modeling of a different standard. No moment where James had said, even kindly: *let's come back to that, Grace, I want to make sure we have time for the next item.*

You couldn't hold someone accountable to a standard they'd never been given.

That wasn't Grace's problem. That was the room's problem. That was the *system's* problem.

The meeting ended at ten-eighteen, which was eighteen minutes past its scheduled close. No one seemed to notice or mind until Will got up and realized he was late to his ten o'clock, which abruptly ended the meeting.

As people filtered out, Jayne sat with her notepad and let the room empty.

James caught her eye on his way out and gave her a look that asked: *well?*

She gave him a small nod that said: *we'll talk.*

She looked back down at her notes. Five people. One table. Approximately sixty minutes of conversation.

What she had seen was not a broken team. That was the thing she always had to remind herself — and sometimes remind her clients — in these early moments.

A broken team looked different. A broken team had open hostility, or checked-out silence, or the kind of corrosive cynicism that told you trust had left the building a long time ago.

This team was none of those things.

This team was thoughtful and capable and, in their way, genuinely trying.

But something wasn't working. You could feel it in the unfinished decisions and the careful diplomacy and the way the meeting had ended without anyone being quite sure what, specifically, was going to happen next. There was warmth in that room. There was intelligence.

What there wasn't, yet, was forward movement.

Jayne capped her pen and gathered her things and walked out into the hallway, already thinking about where to start.

CHAPTER FIVE

The Engagement Begins

James's office had the kind of lived-in quality that told you something about a person.

Not messy — organized, actually, in the way that people who move fast tend to organize things: stacks with internal logic, a whiteboard with half-erased diagrams that had probably been important two weeks ago, a bookshelf that mixed business titles with a few worn paperbacks and a youth soccer trophy that had no business being in a CEO's office but felt completely right in here.

There was a photo on the credenza behind his desk. A younger James — maybe fifteen years younger — standing in front of a much smaller building with a small group of people, all of them squinting into the sun and grinning. Jayne looked at it while she waited for him to finish a call.

She could pick out Grace immediately. Same smile, same posture, same complete unselfconsciousness in front of a camera. Standing right next to James.

He hung up and followed her gaze.

"Day we moved into our first real office," he said. "Twelve people. We ordered pizza and ate it on the floor because we didn't have furniture yet."

"How many of them are still here?"

He looked at the photo for a moment. "Three. Me, Grace, and our head of accounting." A pause. "Frank retired last year, actually. So just the two of us now." He shifted slightly. "Olivia actually replaced Frank. We decided we needed to elevate the role from head of accounting to CFO."

Jayne smiled quietly to herself and made a mental note. *Elevated the role.* It was a small phrase, but it told her something — about how James narrated change, about what he chose to frame as growth versus what might also have been a pattern of restructuring around people rather than addressing things directly.

He said it without apparent significance. Jayne didn't point any out.

"Tell me how you felt about this morning," she said.

James settled into his chair. He had the habit of leaning back slightly when he was thinking and forward slightly when he'd made up his mind, and right now he was somewhere in between.

"Honestly? Normal. That was a pretty normal meeting for us."

"What does normal look like for you and Meridian?" Jayne asked.

James thought for a moment. "Status quo. Everyone shows up, does their job. Nothing is on fire. Nothing earth-shattering happening either."

Jayne let the silence sit. She'd learned a long time ago that the space after an answer like that was where the real thinking happened — the moment when a leader heard their own words played back by the quiet in the room.

"Is normal working?" she asked.

He looked at her. "If it were working, you wouldn't be here."

She smiled. "Fair."

Another pause. James seemed to weigh something, then redirected.

"So tell me what you saw."

"I'll get there," Jayne said. "But I want to talk about next steps first, because I think the sequence matters."

She opened her bag and set a single sheet of paper on the desk between them — a simple one-pager she'd drafted that morning. "Here's what I'm recommending."

He leaned forward to read it.

She walked him through it plainly. She and three colleagues would work with the full leadership team individually — one-on-one coaching, starting immediately. But before any of that started, she wanted to conduct 360-degree feedback assessments across the entire team. Anonymous input from direct reports, peers, clients or business partners if possible, and the leadership team members themselves. Structured. Confidential. Real.

"The 360 gives us a baseline," she said. "It tells us what the organization is actually experiencing — not what we assume it's experiencing. And it gives each leader something concrete to work with. A mirror, essentially."

"And then?"

"And then we use what we learn to shape the annual planning session. I'd facilitate it. Not just as a strategy exercise or a fun retreat — but as a team development experience. The goal is to walk out of that room with a real plan. Not a deck. A plan — and some individual and team awareness."

James nodded slowly. He'd been nodding through most of it, which she'd already identified as a pattern worth watching.

"I want to do the 360s on everyone," she said. "The full leadership team."

"Including Grace?"

"Including everyone," she said. "Including you."

There it was — the same moment as the phone call, slightly reloaded. James held it for a second.

"You mentioned that on the call," he said.

"I did. I'm mentioning it again because it's the part that matters most and the part most leaders would prefer to quietly negotiate their way out of."

He almost smiled. "Is that your way of telling me not to try?"

"It's my way of telling you that the 360 on *you* is going to be the most useful data in the room. Because whatever we learn about your team, the context for all of it is what's happening at the top." She held his gaze. "That's not an indictment. That's just how systems work."

James was quiet for a moment. Outside the glass walls of his office, the floor hummed with the ordinary activity of a Tuesday morning — keyboards, conversations, someone laughing near the kitchen. The company he had built, going about its business.

"What if it says things I don't agree with?" he asked.

It was a more honest question than most people asked at this stage. She gave it a straight answer.

"Then we talk about that too. Feedback isn't a verdict. It's a data point. But James—" She paused, making sure she had his full attention. "In my experience, when a leader doesn't agree with their 360 feedback, that itself is worth paying attention to."

He held her gaze for a moment. Then something in him settled — not resigned, but decided. The forward lean.

"Okay," he said. "Let's do the whole thing. All of it."

"Good." She picked up the one-pager and slid it back into her bag. "One more thing."

"What's that?"

"When you talk to the team about this — and you should talk to them today, before word gets around on its own — I'd encourage you to frame this as an investment. In them. In the team. In the company. Not as a response to any individual performance concern."

She watched him carefully as she said it.

He nodded. "Because if I frame it around Grace—"

"She'll know. They'll all know. And you'll have a trust problem before we've even started."

James looked at the photo on the credenza again. Just for a second.

"She's going to know anyway," he said quietly. "She's been here long enough. She knows when something's up."

"Maybe," Jayne said. "But there's a difference between someone sensing that change is coming and feeling like they've been identified as the problem. One of those people can still engage openly. The other one gets defensive. And a defensive Grace isn't going to get you what you need out of this process."

He nodded. This time it felt like something more than a reflex.

"I'll talk to them this afternoon," he said.

"Good." Jayne stood, gathered her bag. "And James?"

He looked up.

"When you have that conversation — try to mean it. The part about it being an investment. Because I think it actually is."

He held that for a moment. Then, quietly, he said: "Even for Grace?"

Jayne looked at him evenly. "Especially for Grace."

She had three missed calls by the time she reached the parking lot — her colleague Marcus, following up on another engagement, and two she'd return later. She sat in her car for a minute before starting the engine.

She thought about the photo on James's credenza. Twelve people on the floor of an empty office, eating pizza and squinting into the sun. The kind of founding moment that becomes mythology inside a company — the story people tell when they want to remember why they built the thing in the first place.

Grace was in that photo.

Which meant that whatever came next — whatever the 360s revealed, whatever the work uncovered, however this engagement ultimately resolved — Grace Matthews wasn't just an employee with performance issues. She was part of the origin story. She carried the memory of what this company had been before it became what it was.

That mattered. It complicated things. It made the work more delicate and, Jayne thought, more important.

She started the engine.

The easy version of this engagement would be to confirm what James already believed, give Grace some coaching that didn't quite take hold, and let the organization reach its own inevitable conclusions. Jayne had seen other consultants do that. It was cleaner. It was faster. It preserved the relationship with the CEO and let everyone feel like they'd tried.

She wasn't interested in the easy version.

She pulled out of the parking lot and into traffic, already composing in her head the notes she'd send to her colleagues that evening. There was a lot of work to do before anyone sat down with a 360 questionnaire.

She had a feeling the data was going to be very interesting.

ACT TWO: THE MIRROR

CHAPTER SIX

What They Said About Grace

The 360 process, when it's done well, is one of the most clarifying tools in organizational work. When it's done poorly, it's a weapon.

Jayne had seen both. She'd seen 360s used to build a case for termination before the leader being assessed ever saw the data. She'd seen them delivered in a single meeting, raw and unfiltered, and watched the recipient shut down so completely that nothing useful happened for months afterward. She'd seen organizations treat 360 feedback the way some people treat annual physicals — something you schedule because you're supposed to, endure because you have to, and forget about by the following Tuesday.

She had no intention of doing any of that.

Her process was structured but human. She and her team of coaches conducted the interviews— all of them, for every leader. No online surveys. No multiple-choice questionnaires with a comment box at the bottom. Just conversations. Forty-five minutes each, sometimes longer, with direct reports, peers, clients when possible, and the leadership team members themselves.

They asked the same five questions in every interview. Jayne had refined them over years and they were deceptively simple:

What does this leader do that makes the team or organization better?

What gets in the way of this leader being as effective as they could be?

If you could change one thing about how this leader shows up, what would it be?

What does this leader not see about themselves?

Is there anything you've been wanting to tell this leader but haven't?

The last question was the one that mattered most. It was also the one that took the longest to answer, because most people in organizations have been trained — by experience, by culture, by survival instinct — to hold back the thing they most want to say.

Jayne gave them permission to say it. And then she listened.

Grace's feedback came in first, partly because Jayne had Marcus start the interview process with the people around Grace — her direct reports in HR, the leaders she supported, a few long-tenured employees who had worked with her for years.

The themes were clear. They were also, Jayne noted, almost exactly what James had described.

Her direct reports respected her. They used words like *loyal* and *dedicated* and *always willing to go to bat for her team.* One of them said she was the reason he'd stayed at Meridian through two different moments when he'd considered leaving. Another said Grace had personally mentored her through the hardest year of her career.

That part was real. It mattered. Jayne underlined it twice in her notes.

But then the other side of the picture emerged.

She talks more than she listens. She's slow to act on things that feel urgent to us. She has a hard time letting go of how things used to be done. She doesn't always read the room. She gets defensive when she feels challenged, even when the challenge is constructive.

The peers — Olivia, Alex, Will — were more pointed, though each in their own way.

Olivia was precise: "I respect her institutional knowledge, but when I need a decision or a candidate, the process takes twice as long as it should. I've started going around her when I can, which I know isn't great."

Alex was direct but careful, in the way of someone who was very conscious of his position in the company: "Grace and I see the world differently. That's not a bad thing. But she has a way of framing everything through the lens of how it's always been done, and when you're trying to build something new, that's hard to work with."

Will was the most diplomatic, which didn't surprise Jayne at all: "Grace is one of the most genuine people I've ever worked with. She cares deeply. I just think she sometimes lets that caring get in the way of seeing what's actually needed." He paused. "And I don't think anyone has ever really told her that directly. Including me."

That last sentence, Jayne thought, was the most honest thing anyone had said in the entire Grace feedback process.

She compiled it all into a report — organized by theme, anonymized, with direct quotes where they were illustrative and her own synthesis where context was needed. It was thorough but not clinical. She wanted the data to feel like it came from real people, because it did.

She set it aside and moved on to the next set of interviews.

James's.

CHAPTER SEVEN

What They Said About James

The feedback on James started the way Jayne expected it would.

Everyone liked him.

That wasn't performance — it was genuine. Direct reports, peers, even the senior stakeholders she spoke with: James Wilson was respected. Admired, even. He was the kind of leader people wanted to work for, the kind who remembered your kid's name and asked about your mother's surgery and meant it when he said his door was always open.

One of his direct reports put it this way: "James is the reason most of us are here. Not the company. Not the stock. James."

Jayne wrote it down and felt the weight of it. Being that loved by your organization was a gift. It was also, in her experience, a trap.

Because the rest of the feedback told a different story.

Not a contradictory story — that would have been simpler. A *parallel* story. One that lived right alongside the admiration and existed in the same breath.

The first theme was clarity — or, more precisely, the lack of it.

I'm never quite sure what we're actually trying to accomplish in a given quarter. The priorities seem to shift depending on what meeting you're in.

He has a vision, but it changes. Sometimes week to week. And when it changes, he doesn't always tell us — we just figure it out when we realize the thing we were working on isn't the thing anymore.

I've stopped putting too much energy into long-term plans because I know they'll probably be different in six weeks.

That last one stopped Jayne for a moment. It was almost word for word what she'd said on the podcast — the same pattern she'd described with another CEO, another company, another version of the same story. The parallel made her careful. She didn't want to project an old engagement onto a new one. But the data was the data.

The second theme was decisiveness.

James asks for everyone's input, which is great. But then he asks again. And again. At some point you realize he's not gathering information — he's avoiding a decision.

We had a conversation about the reorg in March. And April. And June. And September. Nothing has actually been decided.

He's the nicest person I've ever worked for and the hardest person to get a clear answer from.

The third theme was accountability.

When someone doesn't deliver, nothing happens. There's no consequence. So why would anyone change?

He wants everyone to like him. And I get it — he's likable. But sometimes you need your CEO to be clear, not nice. Or at least clear first and nice second.

His say/do ratio is lower than he thinks it is. He commits to things in meetings and then either forgets or quietly changes course, and nobody calls him on it because — well, because he's James.

Jayne sat with that phrase for a long time. *Because he's James.* It had the quality of a cultural artifact — something that had been repeated so often it had become part of the operating system. Everybody understood what it meant. Nobody questioned it.

That, she thought, was exactly the kind of thing a system builds around a leader without the leader ever asking for it.

There was one more thread in the feedback that Jayne hadn't expected, though in retrospect she should have.

It was about Alex.

Not about Alex directly — nobody had anything critical to say about his performance. But several people, unprompted, raised the dynamic of having the CEO's son as COO. The concern wasn't that Alex was unqualified. It was that nobody was sure what the rules were.

Does Alex report to James the way the rest of us do? Or is there a different conversation happening at home?

I like Alex. He's sharp. But I don't always know if I'm talking to my peer or to the future CEO.

James created that role for Alex. He says it was about strategy, but I think it was about succession. And that's fine — I just wish someone would say it out loud.

Jayne noted the pattern: the organization wanted clarity about Alex the same way it wanted clarity about everything else. Not because people were hostile to the idea of succession. Because nobody had named it. And in the absence of naming, people fill the space with their own assumptions.

She closed her notebook and looked at the full picture.

James Wilson was loved by his company. He was also, in ways he couldn't yet see, the primary author of almost every frustration his team had described.

The unclear strategy was his. The shifting priorities were his. The accountability gap was his. The avoidance of hard decisions was his. Even the issue with Grace — the one he'd called Jayne about in the first place — was, in part, a product of a system that had never required Grace to be different, because the person at the top had never been willing to hold the line.

He was a good man running a good company. They would not have employed 500 people and made $180M if there were not good things happening, but it also felt like the company was in a holding pattern, and James was eager to see the company grow. And he was the problem he couldn't see.

Now she had to tell him.

CHAPTER EIGHT

The Coaching Team

One of the things Jayne had learned early in her career — the hard way, as most important lessons arrive — was that she couldn't do this work alone.

Not because the workload was too heavy, though it often was. Because the perspective got too narrow. When you're deep inside an organization, working closely with a leader, coaching them through real vulnerability, you start to lose the very thing that made you useful in the first place: distance.

That was why she'd built her team the way she had.

There were four of them on the Meridian engagement. Jayne worked with James directly. Marcus Cole, a former HR executive turned coach who had a gift for cutting through organizational politics without making anyone feel exposed, was paired with Grace. Dina Reyes, who specialized in high-potential leaders navigating identity and authority, took Alex. And Tom Sadler, a quiet, deeply experienced coach who had a knack for drawing out people who performed ease while carrying tension, was paired with Will.

Olivia, being eight months in, was in a slightly different position. Jayne had suggested a lighter-touch engagement for now — periodic check-ins rather than a full coaching arc — and had assigned herself to those conversations. Olivia was still observing. She wasn't ready to be coached; she was ready to be heard.

The team met monthly — the coaches, not the clients. It was a practice Jayne had instituted years ago and considered non-negotiable. They gathered on a video call, shared what they were seeing, and helped each other think.

The rules were simple: everything stayed confidential to the coaching team. No one repeated a client's words to another client. They discussed themes and patterns, not private disclosures. And they were honest with each other, even when it was uncomfortable.

The first full team meeting on the Meridian engagement happened three weeks into the 360 interview process, before any of the feedback had been formally delivered.

Marcus went first.

"Grace is open," he said. "More open than I expected. She knows something is off. She just doesn't have language for it yet." He paused. "She keeps saying things like *'I just need to figure out what they want from me,'* which tells me she's operating from a place of confusion, not resistance. She's not pushing back. She's lost."

"Does she know why she was the original focus of the engagement?" Jayne asked.

"She suspects. She hasn't said it directly, but she's made a few comments about 'being the one who's been here the longest' and 'not always fitting in the way I used to.' There's some grief in it, I think. She's mourning a version of the company that doesn't exist anymore."

Jayne made a note. Grief was useful. Grief meant something real was being processed. Resistance without grief was just defense. Grief without awareness was harder, but it was a starting point.

Dina was next.

"Alex is interesting," she said, in the way she always said *interesting* — meaning complicated. "He's performing at a very high level and he's frustrated because he can't figure out why that isn't enough. He brings prepared recommendations to meetings. They get turned into group discussions. He's starting to internalize that as a signal that his father doesn't trust him, when I think the real issue is that his father doesn't trust *himself* to make a call."

"Is the family dynamic on the table?" Marcus asked.

"Barely. He mentions it obliquely. Says things like 'it's complicated when your boss is also your dad.' He wants to be seen as a leader in his own right. But he's also deeply loyal to James and doesn't want to be the one who names the gap."

"That's going to come up," Jayne said. "At the off site, if not before."

"I know," Dina said. "I'm working on helping him find his own voice for it. Not mine. His."

Tom, as usual, waited until everyone else had spoken.

"Will is charming," he said. "Which is the problem?"

The group laughed — not unkindly. They'd all coached leaders like Will.

"He's the emotional thermostat for the team," Tom continued. "He reads the room better than anyone else at that table and he uses it to keep things smooth. Which means he's also the one making sure certain conversations never actually happen. He's not doing it maliciously. He genuinely believes that's his job — to keep the peace, to find the compromise, to make sure nobody gets too uncomfortable."

"And Grace?" Jayne asked. "The relationship between them."

Tom nodded. "That's real. They're close. He's protective of her in a way that's generous but also limiting. He smooths things over for her in meetings. He translates her points into language the room can receive. Which means she never has to learn to do it herself."

"So he's part of the system that's keeping her stuck," Marcus said.

"Without knowing it. Or at least without framing it that way." Tom leaned back. "The other thing I'm watching is his ambition. He's not talking about it openly, but there's a succession current running under everything. He's been here ten years. He's well-liked. He's wondering whether the path to the top runs through loyalty, succession, or through something more assertive. And he hasn't decided yet."

Jayne shared what she'd been seeing with James and Olivia, careful to keep it at the level of theme rather than detail.

"James is starting to realize the 360 is going to say things he doesn't want to hear," she said. "He's not there yet. He's still holding onto the idea that Grace is the core issue. The feedback is going to challenge that, and I need to be ready for the defensiveness."

"And Olivia?" Dina asked.

"Olivia is the most interesting variable," Jayne said. "She's not entangled in any of the legacy dynamics. She's watching everything with clear eyes. She's also the newest person on that team, which gives her a different vantage point. When she finally decides to speak, it's going to matter."

The call lasted another twenty minutes. They talked about timing — when to deliver the feedback, in what order, how to sequence the individual sessions so that the team arrived at the offsite with enough awareness to make the two days productive but not so much raw emotion that the room became unmanageable.

It was the kind of planning that happened invisibly, behind the scenes, without the client ever seeing it. The choreography of good coaching. Jayne thought of it as setting the table — making sure the right conversations could happen in the right order, so that when the moment arrived, the leader was ready to hear what they needed to hear.

She hung up the call and sat in the quiet of her home office for a moment.

Four leaders. Four coaches. One CEO who was about to discover that the problem he'd called her about was a mirror.

She opened her laptop and began drafting James's feedback report.

CHAPTER NINE

The Feedback Session

Jayne had delivered hundreds of 360 reports in her career. She knew the rhythms of it — the way a leader's face changed as they moved through the data, the predictable sequence of recognition, surprise, and resistance that almost always unfolded in the same order.

James's session followed the pattern almost exactly.

They met in his office on a Thursday afternoon. She'd asked for ninety minutes and told him to clear the time after it, too. "You're going to want space to think," she'd said, and he'd looked at her with the slight wariness of someone who was beginning to understand that this process was going to cost him something.

She started with the positives, because they were real and because he needed to hear them.

"Your team respects you deeply," she said. "That came through in every single interview. You are genuinely liked, James. Not performed-liked, I actually liked it. People feel safe with you. They trust your intentions. That's not nothing — that's the foundation of everything we're going to build on."

He nodded, but she could see he was bracing.

"The concern is not who you are," she continued. "It's what you do — or, in some cases, what you don't do."

She walked him through it theme by theme. The clarity issue first — the shifting strategy, the priorities that changed without announcement. Then the decisiveness piece — the way he gathered input past the point of usefulness, the committee reflex, the pattern of asking what everyone thought when what the room needed was a call. Then accountability — the absence of consequences, the commitments that quietly dissolved, the say/do gap.

She read him selected quotes, anonymized but direct. She watched his face.

He was quiet through most of it. At one point he leaned back in his chair — the thinking posture — and stayed there for a long time.

When he finally spoke, his voice was measured.

"Some of this I've heard before," he said. "The accountability piece. I know I'm not great at that."

"What about the rest?"

He looked at the window. "The strategy thing — I don't think that's fair. Markets change. You have to adapt. If I held a rigid strategy, we'd have missed half the opportunities that got us to $180 million."

"That may be true," Jayne said. "And it's also true that your team doesn't know what they're building toward in any given quarter. Both things can be real at the same time."

He didn't respond to that directly. Instead, he shifted.

"What about Grace?" he asked. "What did her feedback say?"

Jayne had been expecting the redirect. She'd been watching for it.

"Grace's feedback is for Grace," she said. "I'll share themes with you where they're relevant to the team dynamic, but the specifics are between her and Marcus. The same way your feedback is between you and me."

"But you can tell me if it confirmed what I've been saying."

"I can tell you this," Jayne said carefully. "Some of the patterns you described are real. Grace does have development areas that are showing up in the data. She's not landing with the team the way she needs to."

James leaned forward. Relief was already forming on his face.

"But," Jayne said, and she held the word long enough for the relief to pause. "The data also shows something else. Multiple people — not one, not two, *multiple* people — said that Grace has never been given clear, direct feedback about these patterns. Not from her peers. And not from you."

The room got very quiet.

"I've talked to her," James said. "Multiple times."

"I believe you've had conversations," Jayne said. "But there's a difference between a conversation and a clear expectation with a defined consequence. And there's a difference between giving someone feedback and giving someone feedback they can actually hear. The organization is telling me that Grace has been allowed to operate this way for years, and nobody — including you — has drawn a line."

She watched his jaw tighten.

"That's the system, James. That's what I keep coming back to. Grace isn't operating in a vacuum. She's operating in the system you've built. A system where expectations are unclear, where accountability is soft, and where the person at the top avoids the hard conversation until it becomes a crisis." She paused. "Grace may be struggling. But she's struggling inside a structure that was never set up for her to succeed."

James was quiet for a long time. Jayne didn't fill the silence.

"I don't agree with all of this," he said finally.

"I know."

"I think you're letting her off the hook."

"I'm not letting anyone off the hook. Including you."

He met her eyes. There was something happening behind them — not anger exactly, but the discomfort of being seen in a way he hadn't invited.

"So what do we do?" he asked.

"We go to the off-site," Jayne said. "And we see if the team can do something different. But James — the offsite isn't just about getting alignment on strategy. It's about whether this team can actually operate differently. And that starts with you."

He nodded. Slowly. The kind of nod that wasn't agreement yet but was no longer refusal either.

"You said I should have space after this," he said.

"I did."

"I think I'm going to go for a drive."

Jayne gathered her things and let herself out. She didn't look back.

Some things need to land in silence.

CHAPTER TEN

The Bad Meeting

Three weeks later, the leadership team met for their standing Tuesday session, and Jayne wasn't there.

She'd made a deliberate choice not to attend. The 360s had been delivered to every leader individually by this point. Each of them had sat with their data. Each of them was in the early, tender phase of absorbing what their colleagues and their organization had actually said about them. Jayne wanted to see what happened when the team came together under those conditions without a facilitator in the room.

She got the answer by four o'clock that afternoon, when James called her.

"It was bad," he said.

He was in his car. She could hear the engine and the particular quality of someone speaking through a Bluetooth connection while driving slightly too fast.

"Tell me."

"We were supposed to talk about Q4 priorities. Prep for the retreat. Instead, it turned into — I don't even know what to call it. Everyone was talking past each other. Grace brought up a hiring timeline and Alex pushed back, and normally Will would have smoothed it over, but this time he just sat there. Olivia said something about needing clearer metrics and nobody responded. It felt like five people in the same room having five different meetings."

"What did you do?"

A pause. "I asked what everyone thought we should prioritize."

Jayne said nothing.

"I know," James said. "I heard it as soon as I said it. The same thing I always do."

"What happened after that?"

"Nothing. That's the problem. Everyone gave their version of what mattered. Nobody disagreed with anyone. Nobody agreed with anyone either. We ran forty minutes over and I'm not sure we decided a single thing. And then Will had to leave for another meeting and that just — ended it. Again."

Jayne recognized the frustration in his voice, but she also recognized something else: awareness. Three weeks ago, James would have described this meeting as "pretty normal." He wouldn't have called her about it. He wouldn't have noticed the pattern.

The 360 was doing its work. Not by changing his behavior yet — that would take longer — but by changing what he could see.

"James, can I ask you something?"

"Go ahead."

"Three weeks ago, you described your leadership meetings as 'normal.' Status quo. Everyone shows up, does their job, nothing on fire. What you just described to me sounds a lot like that same meeting. What's different now?"

The line was quiet for a moment.

"I am," he said. "I'm different. I'm seeing it now."

"Yes," she said. "You are."

He pulled into what sounded like a parking lot. The engine turned off.

"I want you to run our annual planning session ," he said. "Not just facilitate the strategy piece. The whole thing. I want you to help us figure out how to actually work together, because clearly we don't know how."

"That's what I was going to recommend," she said.

"Of course it was." He almost laughed. "When can we do it?"

"Your annual planning is in three weeks. Let's use it. Two full days, and let's make it an off-site, away from the office. I'll work with you on the agenda, but I want input from the full team and from the coaching team as well."

"What should I tell them?"

"Tell them this year's session is going to be different. Tell them it's not just about strategy. Tell them it's about how this team operates — how you make decisions, how you hold each other accountable, how you communicate. And tell them that everything is on the table."

A pause.

"Including me?" he asked.

It was the same question he'd asked in their first phone call, in his office, and now again here. But it sounded different this time. The first time, it had been a question about whether he was willing. Now it was a question about whether he was ready.

"Especially you," Jayne said.

She picked up her phone and texted Marcus, Dina, and Tom:

Offsite is a go. Three weeks. Let's meet tomorrow to plan. This one matters.

ACT THREE: THE ROOM

CHAPTER ELEVEN

Before the Room

The venue was a conference center forty minutes from Meridian's office — close enough to be practical, far enough to feel like leaving. Jayne had suggested it. She'd learned that the physical distance mattered more than people thought. When a team stayed in their own building, they brought their habits with them. The hallway conversations, the familiar chairs, the inbox glowing on their screens. Getting out — even by forty minutes — broke the pattern just enough to make different conversations possible.

She arrived the evening before, walked the space, rearranged the chairs from classroom-style rows into a U-shape, and taped three sheets of blank paper to the wall. She wrote one question on each:

What would have to be true for this to be the most important two days this company has had in years?

What are we willing to do differently?

What are we afraid to say out loud?

She stepped back and looked at them. The third one was a risk. Some facilitators wouldn't put it up. But Jayne had found that naming the fear in the room — putting it on the wall where everyone could see it — was often the thing that made it safe enough to actually speak.

She left it.

The planning had taken two weeks. She'd worked with James on the agenda, but she'd also collected input from every leader individually and from her coaching team. She wanted the two days to feel like they belonged to the whole team, not just to James and not just to her.

The structure she'd designed was deliberate. Day 1 was about foundation: how the team would work together in the room, what they believed about alignment, and the current state of the company. Day 2 was about decisions: the priorities for the year, the hard conversation about what to stop, and the beginning of real accountability.

She sat in the empty conference room the night before and thought about what she knew.

She knew that James had spent the last three weeks sitting with feedback that challenged his self-image. He was more aware than he'd been, but awareness and behavior change were different animals. She would be watching to see whether the patterns from his 360 showed up in real time — the hedging, the consensus-seeking, the avoidance of hard calls.

She knew that Alex was ready to push. Dina had told her that his coaching sessions had moved from frustration to something more like resolve. He'd been thinking about what it meant to lead in his own right, not as James's son, and the offsite was going to test that.

She knew that Will was going to be the most interesting variable. Tom had flagged something in their last coaching debrief: Will had started to question his own role as the team's smoother. "He's beginning to wonder if being the person who keeps the peace is actually keeping him from being the leader he wants to be," Tom had said. That was progress. It was also volatile. A Will who stopped smoothing might leave a gap the team wasn't ready for.

She knew that Grace was coming in vulnerable but willing. Marcus had done careful work preparing her for the offsite — not coaching her on what to say, but helping her understand what her 360 data actually meant and how to be present in the room without reverting to old patterns. But Jayne had also seen enough to know that preparation and performance were different things. The offsite would put Grace under real pressure, in real time, in front of the people whose opinions mattered most to her. There was no rehearsal for that.

And she knew that Olivia was a wild card. Quiet, observant, quiet, observant — and increasingly frustrated by what she was seeing. When Olivia finally decided to speak her mind in front of the group, it would carry unusual weight. Jayne just didn't know when that moment would come.

She turned off the lights and left the room exactly as it was.

Tomorrow, five leaders would walk through that door carrying everything they'd been given over the past six weeks — data, coaching, questions, discomfort. Her job was to create a container strong enough to hold all of it.

She went back to her room and opened her notebook to review the Day 1 agenda one more time.

CHAPTER TWELVE

Day One Morning: The Foundation

They arrived in the order Jayne might have predicted.

Olivia was first, fifteen minutes early, with a coffee and a clean notebook. She sat down, looked at the three questions on the wall, and read them without expression. Then she opened her notebook and wrote something.

Alex came next, five minutes early, carrying a laptop bag and the slightly coiled energy of someone who had prepared for something and was ready for it to start.

Will arrived exactly on time, with coffee for himself and a pastry for the table. He scanned the room, clocked the U-shaped chairs, and took a seat that put him in the middle of one arm — visible to everyone, next to no one in particular.

Grace walked in two minutes late, slightly flustered, carrying her travel mug and the three-ring binder. She looked around the room, seemed momentarily uncertain about where to sit, and chose the chair closest to Will.

James was last. Three minutes late. He paused at the door, looked at the room, and Jayne saw him make a small, conscious choice. Instead of taking the seat at the head of the U — the natural power position — he sat on the arm opposite Will, between Alex and Olivia.

Whether he'd done it intentionally or instinctively, Jayne noted it. It was a different choice than he would have made six weeks ago.

"Good morning," Jayne said. "Before we do anything else, I want to start with something simple. I'd like us to agree on how we're going to work together for the next two days."

She put a flip chart at the front of the room and wrote Working Session Agreements at the top.

"These aren't rules," she said. "They're commitments. And they only work if everyone in this room owns them. So I'm going to suggest a few and then I want to hear from you."

She wrote the first one: *Be present. Devices off unless we're on a break.*

Nods around the room. Easy.

Second: *Say what you mean. If you disagree, say so in this room, not in the parking lot after.*

Fewer nods. Will shifted slightly in his chair.

Third: *Alignment does not require agreement.*

She let that one sit.

"What does that mean, exactly?" Alex asked.

"It means you don't have to agree with every decision this team makes. But once a decision is made, you align behind it. You support it publicly. You execute on it. And if you have a problem with it, you bring it back to this room — not to your own team, not to the hallway, not to a side conversation with one person."

"So we're supposed to just go along with things we don't believe in?" Grace asked. There was genuine confusion in her voice, not challenge.

"No," Jayne said. "You're supposed to fight for what you believe in — *in this room.* Make your case. Push back.

Disagree openly. And then, when the team decides, you commit to the decision. Even if it wasn't your preference."

"That only works if the decision is actually clear," Olivia said quietly.

It was the first time she'd spoken in the session. Every head turned.

"You're right," Jayne said. "It only works if someone makes the call. Which brings me to the next thing I want to introduce."

She explained Fist to Five.

The concept was simple: when the team needed to make a decision, everyone would hold up a hand. A fist meant *I cannot support this and will actively oppose it.* One finger meant *I have serious concerns.* Three means *I can live with it.* Five meant *I fully support it and will champion it.*

"The key," Jayne said, "is that a three or above means you're in. You may not love it, but you're committing to it. And a two or below means we stop and talk about it. No one gets steamrolled and no one gets to silently disagree."

"What if James overrides the group?" Alex asked. He said it casually, but the question had weight.

James looked at his son. "I'm not going to —"

"Actually," Jayne said, "that's a fair question. And the honest answer is: sometimes the CEO does need to make a final call that the room doesn't fully agree with. That's part of the job. The difference is transparency. If James makes a call, he says so. He explains why. And the team aligns behind it, because that's what alignment means."

She looked at James. "The question for you is whether you're willing to actually do that. Not defer to consensus. Not ask what everyone thinks. Make the call."

The room was very still.

"Yes," James said. "I'm willing to try."

"Trying is good," Jayne said. "We'll practice today."

She moved them into an icebreaker that looked, on the surface, like a game.

She held up a tennis ball. "Stand up. Form a circle. The goal is to pass this ball through every person's hands in the fastest time possible. You can't skip anyone. You can't drop it. Go."

They stood. They arranged themselves. James immediately said "okay, so should we go clockwise or—" and Will said "let's just start and figure it out" and Alex said "wait, let's think about this for a second" and Grace said "we used to do something like this at the old office" and Olivia just held out her hands.

The first round took fourteen seconds. Messy. One near-drop.

"Again," Jayne said. "Faster."

Alex took charge. "Tighter circle. Everyone hold your hands like this. Ready?"

Eight seconds.

"Again."

This time Will suggested they stack their hands in a column and let the ball roll through. Grace laughed and said "that's cheating" and Olivia said "she didn't say we couldn't" and they tried it.

Three seconds.

Jayne let them sit back down, breathing a little harder, the energy in the room noticeably different than it had been ten minutes earlier.

"So what just happened?" she asked.

"We got faster," Alex said.

"How?"

"Someone took the lead," Olivia said. And then, with the slightest smile: "It wasn't James."

The room laughed. James laughed too, genuinely, and Jayne saw something pass across his face that looked like relief.

"That's exactly right," Jayne said. "You got faster when someone made a decision, when the rest of you committed to it, and when you stopped debating and started executing. That's the whole workshop in thirty seconds."

She let the point land.

"Now let's see if you can do it with something that actually matters."

CHAPTER THIRTEEN

State of the Union

Jayne had spent an hour with James the previous week preparing for this moment.

"You're going to open Day 1 with a State of the Union," she'd told him. "Fifteen minutes. No slides. Just you, telling this team where the company is, where it needs to go, and what's not working. Be honest. Be specific. And don't ask them what they think until you've finished saying what *you* think."

He'd pushed back on the last part. "That feels like I'm not being collaborative."

"You're not being collaborative," she'd said. "You're being the CEO. They need to hear your perspective before they add theirs. Otherwise you're asking them to lead the conversation you should be leading."

He'd written notes. She'd reviewed them. They were good but safe, and she'd pushed him to go further in two places: naming the revenue shortfall with a specific number, and naming the execution culture problem without softening it.

Now he stood at the front of the room, no laptop, no slides, just a single index card in his hand that she knew he wouldn't look at because he'd memorized it.

"We're at $178 million," he said. "We were supposed to be at $195 million by the end of this year. We're not going to get there. And I want to talk about why, because I don't think we've been honest about it."

The room was attentive. This was a different James than the one who usually opened meetings.

"We have a strategy problem, but it's not that we don't have a strategy. It's that we have too many. Every quarter, we're chasing something slightly different. I know some of that is on the market. But a lot of it is on me. I've changed direction too often and I haven't been clear enough about what actually matters."

Jayne watched the room. Alex sat very still. Olivia's pen was poised but motionless. Will's face was neutral, watching. Grace was looking at James with an expression Jayne couldn't quite read — surprise, maybe, or something adjacent to it.

"We also have an execution problem," James continued. "We make decisions in meetings and then nothing happens. Or things happen, but they're different things than what we decided. And part of that is because I haven't held the line. I've let things slide because I didn't want to have hard conversations."

He paused. Jayne could see the effort it took.

"And I have a leadership problem. Not with any of you individually — I mean with how we work together as a team. We're in silos. We're polite when we should be direct. We agree in the room and disagree in the hallway. And I've let that be okay for too long because it was easier than confronting it."

He looked at Jayne. She gave him the smallest nod.

"So these two days aren't about making a slide deck. They're about deciding three things that actually matter for next year, owning them, and committing to doing the hard work of actually following through. Together."

He sat down.

The room was quiet in a way that felt different from the usual quiet. This wasn't the silence of people waiting to be called on. It was the silence of people processing something that had shifted.

Jayne let it breathe for a full ten seconds.

"Thank you, James," she said. Then, to the room: "What landed for you?"

Alex spoke first. "The part about changing direction too often. I've felt that, but I've never heard you say it."

"The execution piece," Olivia said. "I've only been here eight months, but I've already seen three initiatives start and stall. It's not a people problem. It's a follow-through problem."

Will nodded slowly but didn't speak yet.

Grace was quiet. Then she started to say something — and Jayne could see it coming, the familiar pattern: the deep breath, the lean forward, the beginning of a long preamble rooted in history. "You know, when we first started Meridian, James and I used to sit in his office every Friday and talk about—"

She stopped. Mid-sentence. Something crossed her face — a flash of awareness, almost like catching your reflection unexpectedly. She closed her mouth. Opened it again.

"I think James is right," she said. Just that. Five words.

The room didn't react visibly. But Jayne saw Will glance at Grace with something that looked like surprise, and she saw Grace's hand tighten on her pen.

It had cost her something to stop herself. Jayne didn't know if anyone else in the room could see that, but she could.

"Good," Jayne said. "That's where we start."

CHAPTER FOURTEEN

The Strategy Problem

Jayne gave them the assignment after lunch.

"By the end of today, this team is going to identify no more than three strategic priorities for the next twelve months. Three. Not five. Not seven. Three things that, if you get them right, make the year a success."

She gave each of them a pad of sticky notes and a marker. "Write down what you think the top priorities should be. One per note. Don't edit. Don't filter. Don't look at what anyone else is writing."

They wrote. Jayne collected the notes and put them on the wall.

There were twenty-three.

She stepped back and let the group look.

Some of them overlapped. Revenue growth and market expansion were variations of the same impulse. Talent acquisition and culture improvement were adjacent. Technology modernization appeared three times in slightly different languages.

But some of them didn't overlap at all. Grace had written to preserve *client relationships through leadership transitions*. Alex had written *operational efficiency and cost structure*. Will had written *brand repositioning for the next stage of growth*. Olivia had written two words: *financial discipline*.

James had written four notes. All of them were about growth.

What happened next was exactly what Jayne had expected and exactly what the 360 feedback had predicted.

They talked. They discussed. They explored. They built on each other's ideas with genuine intelligence and good will. It was, in many ways, an impressive conversation. These were smart, experienced leaders who cared about the company.

And after ninety minutes, they had made zero decisions.

Every time someone pushed toward a priority, someone else offered a caveat. Every time a theme started to crystallize, a new consideration was introduced. James, true to form, asked what everyone thought at least four times. Will reframed competing ideas into language that sounded like consensus but wasn't. Alex made a clear recommendation early and then backed off it when Grace raised a concern about implementation timing.

Jayne watched it all.

She watched Olivia write in her notebook and then close it. She watched Will look at James after every exchange, reading the temperature. She watched Alex lean back in his chair with the same almost-imperceptible expression she'd seen in the Fishbowl meeting — the look of someone who had come prepared for a decision and gotten a discussion.

And then she watched Grace.

Grace had been trying. Jayne could see it — the effort to be shorter, to hold back, to let others finish. For the first forty minutes, it worked. Grace listened more than she spoke. She asked a question instead of offering a monologue. She was doing the thing Marcus had been coaching her to do.

But forty minutes was apparently the limit.

When the discussion turned to client retention — Grace's territory, her history, the thing she knew best — the old pattern reasserted itself with the quiet force of a tide coming in. She started with a relevant point about the relationship between talent quality and client satisfaction. It was good. It was useful.

And then she kept going. She moved from the point of view of the context to the history to an anecdote about a client from 2017 to a tangent about how the company's values had shifted since the early days. The room's attention began to drift. Alex looked at his phone. Will started to compose his bridging language. Olivia's pen stopped.

Jayne waited. Part of her wanted to intervene — a gentle redirect, a facilitator's pivot. But she also knew that this was data. The room needed to feel this pattern in real time, and Grace needed to be in it when it happened.

It was James who stopped it.

"Grace," he said. Not unkindly, but clearly. "I want to make sure we have time to get to the decision. Can you land the point?"

The room went still. James had never — in Jayne's observation, *never* — redirected Grace publicly.

Grace's face changed. For a moment, Jayne thought she might push back, or explain, or retreat into hurt. Instead, something more complicated happened. Grace looked at James, then at the table, then back at James. Her mouth tightened. She nodded once.

"The point is that client retention has to be tied to talent quality," she said. "That's it."

It was clipped. It was not graceful. But it was short, and it was clear, and the room moved forward.

Jayne made a note: *James redirected Grace. Cost something for both of them. Watch what happens next.*

At three-fifteen, after another thirty minutes of circular discussion, Jayne stood up.

"Stop," she said.

The room went quiet.

"I want to name what I'm seeing," she said. "Not to embarrass anyone. Because I think you're all doing exactly what you know how to do — and that's the problem."

She walked to the wall of sticky notes.

"You've been talking for ninety minutes. You've generated great ideas. You've been collaborative and respectful and thorough. And you haven't decided anything."

She let that land.

"This is the pattern your organization described in the 360 feedback. This is what your people see. Not a team that doesn't care, but a team that can't commit. And the reason you can't commit is that committing to something means *not* committing to something else, and nobody in this room wants to be the person who says no."

Will shifted in his chair. Grace was looking at her hands — still processing the redirect from James, Jayne thought. Alex was staring at the wall of sticky notes.

Jayne turned to James.

"James. You have twenty-three ideas on this wall. Your team needs three. I'm asking you to pick them. Right now. The room held its breath.

CHAPTER FIFTEEN

The Crack

James didn't stand up right away.

He sat for a moment, looking at the wall. Jayne could see him doing what he always did — running the options, weighing the perspectives, trying to find the answer that would satisfy everyone.

Then something shifted. She could see it in his posture. The forward lean.

He stood.

He walked to the wall and was quiet for about fifteen seconds, which in a room that tense felt like a full minute. Then he pulled three sticky notes off the wall and stuck them, spaced apart, on a clean section.

"Revenue growth through deepening existing client relationships — not new markets. Operational efficiency and cost structure. And technology modernization to support both."

He turned around.

"That's where we focus."

The room was silent.

Will spoke first, carefully. "What about brand repositioning? We've been talking about that for a year."

"It's important," James said. "But it's not in the top three. Not this year. We can't do everything."

Will nodded. Slowly. It wasn't an enthusiastic agreement, but it was acceptance.

Alex was next. "I agree with the operational efficiency piece. But I think the way you've framed the revenue priority is too conservative. Deepening existing relationships is important, but if we don't expand into at least one adjacent market, we're leaving growth on the table."

Jayne watched James.

The old James would have opened it to the room. Would have said, *That's a good point, what does everyone think?* Would have invited the discussion that would undo the decision.

This James held.

"I hear you," he said. "And I thought about that. But the data is telling us that we're losing existing clients because we're stretched too thin. If we expand before we solidify, we're building on a cracked foundation. We get the base right first. Then we expand."

Alex's jaw tightened. He didn't look at Jayne. He didn't look at the room. He looked directly at his father.

"You're wrong," he said.

Not, *I disagree.* Not, *I see it differently.You're wrong.*

The room froze. Jayne felt the temperature drop.

James's face tightened. For a moment Jayne saw something she hadn't seen before — not the affable CEO, not the consensus-seeker, but the founder. The man who had built this company from twelve people and a dream. And that man did not appreciate being told he was wrong by his twenty-nine-year-old son in front of his entire leadership team.

"Alex," James said, and his voice had an edge Jayne hadn't heard before. "I've made the call."

The silence that followed was the hardest kind — the kind where everyone is calculating what to do and nobody wants to move first.

Alex stared at his father for a long moment. Then he pushed his chair back from the table, stood up, and walked out of the room.

He didn't slam the door. He just left.

Jayne let five seconds pass. Then ten.

James was still standing by the wall of sticky notes. His face had gone from hard to something else — not regret exactly, but the particular disorientation of a person who has just done something new and doesn't know yet whether it was right.

"Let's take ten minutes," Jayne said.

The room dispersed. Will went to the coffee table. Olivia stayed in her seat, writing. Grace stood but didn't go anywhere — she hovered near her chair, looking at the door Alex had walked through.

Jayne found Alex outside, leaning against the wall of the hallway with his arms crossed.

"That wasn't my best moment," he said before she could speak.

"No," she said. "It wasn't."

He was quiet.

"But what you said isn't wrong," she continued. "You may have a legitimate strategic disagreement with your father. The issue isn't the disagreement. It's the word 'wrong' and the way you delivered it. That's a son challenging a father, not a COO challenging a CEO."

He flinched. Just slightly.

"You walked out of the room. That means your team just watched you choose not to align. And now every person in there is wondering whether the working agreements we spent an hour building are real or performative."

"So what do I do?"

"You go back in. You say you disagree with the decision but you're committing to it. And you mean it. That's what alignment looks like when it's hard."

He looked at her for a long moment. She could see the effort it took — the pride, the frustration, the genuine belief that he was right about the market, all of it wrestling with the thing he knew he had to do.

"Okay," he said. And he went back in.

Alex sat down. The room was still settling from the break, but everyone was watching him.

"I owe this group an apology," he said. "I disagree with the revenue priority. I want that on the record. But the way I said it was wrong, and walking out was worse. I'm aligned. I'm in. And I'd like to revisit the market expansion question at the end of Q1 with data."

James looked at his son. Something passed between them — not resolution, not forgiveness exactly, but the quiet acknowledgment that they had both just survived something they hadn't been prepared for.

"End of Q1," James said. "With data. We'll put it on the calendar."

Jayne let the room settle. It wasn't settled — not really. The father-son tension was still there, bruised and tender. Alex's apology was genuine but it hadn't erased the moment, and it wouldn't. That was going to live in this team's memory for a while.

But they had a decision. Three priorities. And they'd survived the first real test of the working agreements.

"Let's Fist to Five the three priorities," Jayne said.

Hands went up. One four. Two threes. One five. And Alex: a three, held up with visible effort.

Olivia was the five.

"We're in," Jayne said. "Now let's figure out what each of these actually means."

But the energy in the room had changed. Not broken — just honest. The easy camaraderie of the tennis ball exercise felt like hours ago. What was left was something messier, more fragile, and more real.

Jayne made a note: *The crack happened. Not where I expected. Now we see if it holds or breaks.*

CHAPTER SIXTEEN

Day Two: The Hard Conversation

Day 2 started with a quick weather report check-in.

Jayne asked each person to share one word for how they were arriving that morning. She went around the room.

Olivia: "Engaged."

Alex: "Ready." He said it flatly, and Jayne couldn't tell if he meant it or if he was performing recovery.

Will: "Thoughtful."

Grace: "Trying."

James: "Resolved."

"Good," Jayne said. "Let's use the day well."

They spent the first hour reviewing and detailing the three priorities. For each one, Jayne pushed them through a framework: *Who owns it? What does success look like at 90 days? What resources does it require? And who needs to know?*

The conversations were sharper than the day before, but the sharpness had an edge to it that hadn't been there during the morning of Day 1. Yesterday's blow-up between Alex and James was in the room. Nobody mentioned it directly, but it informed everything — the way people chose their words more carefully, the way Alex spoke precisely and without warmth, the way James occasionally looked at his son with an expression that hovered between concern and something more guarded.

Olivia spoke more than she had in any meeting Jayne had observed. She pulled numbers from memory — margins, run rates, headcount costs — and applied them to each priority with a precision that grounded the conversation. Twice, she pushed back on assumptions that the rest of the team had been treating as settled.

"We can't fund all three at the level you're describing," she said at one point. "Not without cutting something. We need to be honest about what that means."

James looked at her. "What do you recommend?"

"Cut first. Prove the model. Then reassess what we can afford."

"Fist to Five?" Jayne said.

Fours and threes around the room. No fists. No twos.

"We cut first," James said.

Jayne moved them to the conversation she'd been saving for last.

"You've decided what to focus on," she said. "Now I need to ask the harder question. What are you going to *stop* doing?"

The energy in the room changed immediately.

"You can't add three major priorities without creating space for them," Jayne continued. "That means something currently on your plates has to come off. Not get deprioritized. Not get pushed to Q3. Stopped."

The silence was heavy in a different way than the earlier silences. This wasn't the silence of processing. This was the silence of protection. Every person at that table had projects and initiatives and commitments that defined their work. Being asked to stop something felt like being asked to give up a piece of their identity.

Jayne let the silence sit.

James spoke first, which she noted. "The geographic expansion we've been exploring. We've spent six months on it and we're not ready. I think we stop."

Alex's face went flat. He didn't move. He didn't speak. Jayne watched him absorb it — the second hit in two days. First the revenue priority. Now his initiative on the stop list.

The room watched him too.

"Alex?" Jayne said.

A long pause. When he spoke, his voice was controlled but not warm. "I hear the rationale. I don't agree with the timing." Another pause. "But I'll align."

It was the right thing to say. It was not the same as meaning it, and everyone in the room knew the difference.

Will suggested pausing the brand repositioning project. "If it's not in the top three, we shouldn't keep spending on it." He said it cleanly, without the diplomatic buffer he'd normally apply to his own recommendation.

Grace was the last to offer. She sat with it for a long time.

"The mentorship program I've been building," she said quietly. "It's good work. It matters. But it's taking time and resources that should probably go to the talent pipeline for the three priorities." She looked at the table. "I don't want to stop it. But I think I have to."

Will reached over and put his hand briefly on her arm. The gesture was small and genuine.

Olivia spoke last. "There are four recurring reports that go to nobody and accomplish nothing. I'd like to eliminate them and redeploy the analyst time toward the technology priority."

"Fist to Five on the full stop list?" Jayne said.

It was the most uneven vote of the retreat. One four. Two threes. One two. And Alex, who held up a single finger.

The room went quiet.

"A one means serious concerns," Jayne said. "Alex, talk to me."

He took a moment. When he spoke, he was looking at the table, not at anyone.

"The geographic expansion represents six months of my work and the work of twelve people on my team. Stopping it isn't just a strategic decision. It's a signal. It tells my team that what they built doesn't matter. And I'm the one who has to deliver that message." He looked up. "I can align on the other stops. I can't champion this one. Not yet. I need to figure out how to do it in a way that doesn't destroy the morale I've spent six months building."

It was honest. It was also not alignment, and the room could feel the difference.

James opened his mouth — to smooth it, Jayne thought, to find the compromise — and then caught himself.

"The expansion stops," James said. "But Alex, I'll work with you on how we communicate it. The work your team did isn't wasted — it's deferred. And we owe them that message from both of us."

Alex held his father's gaze. Something moved behind his eyes — not acceptance, not yet, but the beginning of it.

"Okay," he said. He moved his hand from a one to a two.

Not a three. A two. Jayne noted it.

Grace was also a two. "I can align," she said. "But I want it on the record that stopping the mentorship program isn't free. We're going to feel that in retention."

"Noted," James said. "We'll watch the retention numbers."

Grace moved to a three. Alex stayed at two.

"We have two twos," Jayne said. She looked at the room. "In Fist to Five, a two means we stop and discuss. But we've discussed. And I think what we're hearing from Alex is something different — not a disagreement with the logic, but a real cost that needs to be acknowledged."

She turned to James. "This is a CEO call."

James looked at his son. "The stop list stands. And I'm accountable for helping you manage the fallout. Not later. This week."

Alex nodded once. He didn't move his hand.

Jayne let it be. Not every decision ended with alignment. Some decisions ended with compliance and trust that the process would hold. That wasn't a failure. It was how real teams operated when the stakes were real.

CHAPTER SEVENTEEN

One Word

The last hour of Day 2 was about execution.

Jayne walked them through the cascade: how the three priorities and their 90-day milestones would be communicated to the next level of leadership, and from there to the broader organization. Who would say what. When. In what forum. With what level of detail.

"The plan only matters if the organization knows about it," she said. "And more importantly, if they believe it's real. Your people have seen annual plans before. They've seen retreats produce documents that go on shared drives and never get mentioned again. If you want this to be different, you have to treat the communication as seriously as the decisions themselves."

They spent thirty minutes building the cascade plan. Each leader owned the communication for their area. James would lead an all-hands within two weeks.

It was practical work. It wasn't glamorous. But Jayne knew from experience that the gap between a good offsite and a wasted one was almost always here — in the follow-through that happened in the first two weeks after the room emptied.

At four o'clock, Jayne asked them to put their pens down.

"We're going to close with something simple," she said. "One word. I'm going to go around the room and I want each of you to give me a single word for what you're taking away from these two days. Don't overthink it. Say the first honest thing."

She started with James.

He looked at the whiteboards, now covered in sticky notes and priority frameworks and accountability charts and the three questions she'd taped to the wall the night before.

"Responsibility," he said.

Alex was next. He paused longer than anyone else.

"Frustrated," he said.

The room absorbed it. Nobody tried to fix it.

Will: "Clarity."

Grace: "Exhausted."

Olivia paused. She looked around the room as if deciding something.

"Timely," she said.

Jayne let the words hang in the room. Responsibility. Frustrated. Clarity. Exhausted. Timely. Not the inspirational checkout a motivational speaker would design. Something better: the truth.

She didn't interpret them. She didn't offer a summary or a motivational close. She just let five people sit with what they'd done and what they'd committed to and the messy, tired, uncertain way it felt to have actually done something different.

"Thank you," she said. "All of you. This was real."

They gathered their things. James lingered, looking at the whiteboards. Alex was the first to leave, with a brief nod to the room that was polite but contained no warmth. Grace and Will walked out together, and Jayne watched Grace say something to him — low, private —

and Will nod in a way that looked less like smoothing and more like listening. Olivia was already on her phone.

The room emptied.

Jayne stayed.

She stood in the quiet conference room with its U-shaped chairs and its whiteboards full of decisions and its flip chart of working agreements and the three questions she'd taped to the wall the night before. The third one — *What are we afraid to say out loud?* — was still blank. Nobody had written on it.

But they'd said some of it anyway. Not all of it. Not even most of it. Alex had said something that cracked the room open and then walked out of it. Grace had caught herself and then lost herself and then been caught by someone else. James had made a decision and then watched his son's face and had to decide again whether to hold.

It wasn't clean. It wasn't the offsite Jayne would have designed if she could control every variable. But you can't control people. You can only create the conditions and trust that what needed to happen would happen. She learned that long ago when she used to want every offsite to end on a positive upbeat, almost fairy tale ending, but over time, she realized, the hard work needed to happen and the room and leaders would land where the system needed it to.

She started taking photos of the whiteboards, preserving the work before the venue staff cleared it. She'd transcribe everything tonight and send it to the team by Monday. The plan. The owners. The timelines. The stop list. All of it in writing, because decisions that existed only in memory were decisions that would dissolve.

She thought about each of them.

James, who had stood at the front of the room and made a decision without asking permission. Who had held the line when his son pushed back. Who had then watched that same son walk out, and had to sit with the knowledge that decisiveness came with a cost he hadn't fully anticipated.

Alex, who was angry. Not performatively angry — actually angry. Who had come back into the room because he knew he should, and had said the right words, and was not yet okay. That was going to take time. More time than the coaching engagement might allow.

Will, who had spoken his own mind instead of translating everyone else's. A small shift, but Jayne knew from experience that for someone who had built their identity around keeping the peace, saying what he actually thought was an act of real courage.

Grace, who had tried and partially succeeded and then partially failed and then been redirected by the one person whose redirection would hurt the most. The look on her face when James stopped her — Jayne would remember that for a long time. Grace was doing the work. But the work was going to get harder before it got easier.

And Olivia, who had said *timely* in a way that carried more weight than anyone else's word. Timely because she'd been watching and waiting and this was the first time she'd seen the team attempt something different. Attempt, not achieve. But the attempt mattered.

Jayne peeled the three questions off the wall, folded them, and put them in her bag.

She turned off the lights.

Two days didn't change a team. She knew that better than anyone. Two days created a window — a brief opening where different patterns were possible, where people could see each other and themselves more clearly, where the system could shift just enough to let something new in.

Whether they kept the window open was up to them. Jayne had her doubts. She always did at this stage — the space between the event and the aftermath, when the glow of the offsite meets the gravity of the ordinary.

She walked out to her car, sat for a moment in the parking lot, and opened her phone to text Marcus, Dina, and Tom:

Offsite is done. Some good things happened. Some hard things too. Alex walked out at one point. Grace had a rough moment. James held the line but it cost him. Let's meet in the next week or two — I need to hear what you're seeing before we plan next steps.

She started the engine.

Three priorities. Five leaders. One system that had been shaken loose but not yet rebuilt.

She didn't know if it was enough. She'd find out.

CHAPTER EIGHTEEN

The Coaches Debrief

Two weeks after the offsite, Jayne's coaching team got on a call.

It was a Thursday evening. Marcus was in his home office in Atlanta, a glass of bourbon visible at the edge of the frame. Dina was in her car in a parking garage, having just finished a session with another client. Tom was at his kitchen table, characteristically unhurried, with a mug of tea and a yellow legal pad.

Jayne had sent them a brief summary of the offsite the day after it ended — including the Alex walkout, Grace's rough moment, and the uneven Fist to Five on the stop list. Now she wanted to hear what their clients had actually said about it.

Marcus went first.

"Grace is struggling," he said. Not gently — directly. "The offsite hit her harder than I expected. She felt good about the moment where she named the accountability gap — she keeps coming back to that. But the moment where James redirected her publicly? That's what she's carrying."

"How is she processing it?" Jayne asked.

"Not well, if I'm honest. She alternates between understanding why it happened and feeling humiliated by it. She told me last session that she's been replaying it every night. She knows the feedback is valid. She knows she was going too long. But knowing it and feeling okay about being stopped in front of her peers are two different things."

"Is she pulling back?"

"Yes. She was quieter in the last two team meetings. Noticeably so. Will mentioned it to Tom." Marcus looked at his notes. "She's overcorrecting. Going from too much to almost nothing. That's not sustainable either. I'm working on helping her find the middle, but she's hurt, and hurt people don't calibrate well."

Jayne made a note. This was the risk she'd anticipated. Grace's growth wasn't going to be linear. It was going to look like progress and then regression and then something messier than either.

Dina reported on Alex.

"He's angry," she said. "More than I'd like. The walkout is bothering him — not because he regrets the feeling, but because he regrets the performance. He knows it looked bad. He's embarrassed by it. And the embarrassment is making him rigid."

"Rigid how?"

"He's complying but not engaging. He's doing exactly what the offsite asked him to do — aligning, executing, showing up. But the spirit isn't there. He's performing alignment without buying in, which is exactly the thing we told the team not to do."

"Does he see that?" Jayne asked.

"Partially. He told me last week that he feels like his father chose the company over his recommendation, and that he's trying not to take it personally, and that he's failing at not taking it personally." Dina paused. "The father-son thing is the real issue. Everything else is downstream of it. Until they have an honest conversation about what the COO role actually means — and what succession actually looks like — Alex is going to keep bumping into this."

"That conversation isn't going to happen in the next sixty days," Jayne said.

"No. It's not. And that's okay. Some things take longer than an engagement."

Tom was brief, as always.

"Will is the most encouraging of the four," he said. "He made a real move at the offsite — saying what he actually thought instead of translating for the room. And he's continued doing it in the weeks since. Not perfectly. He still defaults to smoothing about half the time. But he catches himself more often now."

"And the Grace dynamic?" Jayne asked.

"Still close. But there's a tension that wasn't there before. Grace told him after the offsite — in the hallway, on the way out — 'You don't have to protect me anymore.' He didn't know what to do with that. He's proud of her for saying it and unsettled by what it means for his own role. If he's not the protector, what is he?"

"A leader," Dina said.

"That's the idea," Tom said. "He's not there yet. But the direction is right."

Jayne shared her own read on James and Olivia.

"James is in the hardest part of the process," she said. "The offsite went well enough that he's tempted to believe the work is done. But Alex is still cold. Grace is pulling back. The real behavior change hasn't been tested yet by anything genuinely difficult. And I'm not sure he understands that the hardest leadership moments aren't behind him — they're ahead."

"Olivia?"

"Olivia is the most solid. She told me last week that the offsite was the first time she felt like she was part of a real leadership team, not just a collection of smart people who meet on Tuesdays. But she also said something that worried me a little. She said, 'I'm not sure the rest of them will keep it up.' She's watching to see whether this is real or a one-time event. If the team backslides, she's the one most likely to disengage."

Before they hung up, Tom said something that stayed with Jayne.

"The question isn't whether this team changed at the offsite. The question is whether the change survives contact with reality."

"It's going to get hard," Jayne said.

"Yes," Tom said. "It always does."

CHAPTER NINETEEN

Contact with Reality

The first sign that the offsite agreements were being tested came in week three.

Someone restarted the brand repositioning project.

It was a small thing — a vendor contract renewal, a designer re-engaged, a brief that appeared in the marketing team's shared drive. Will hadn't authorized it. One of his directors had, reasoning that "pausing" wasn't the same as "stopping" and that the vendor relationship would be expensive to restart later.

Olivia found it in a budget review and flagged it in the Tuesday meeting.

"We agreed to stop this," she said. Her voice was calm but there was an edge to it. "Three weeks ago. In the room. With Fist to Five."

Will's face reddened. "I didn't authorize —"

"It's your team," Olivia said. "It's your stop."

The room went quiet. This was the test. The exact test Jayne had known would come — the moment when an offsite commitment met the gravitational pull of the ordinary.

James looked at Will.

In the old world — three months ago, before Jayne, before the 360, before the offsite — James would have said something like, *Let's figure out the best path forward as a team.* He would have opened a discussion. He would have found a way to let Will save face.

Instead he said, "Will, kill it. Today. And let me know when it's done."

Will nodded. He didn't argue. He didn't explain. He pulled out his phone under the table and Jayne heard — later, from Tom — that he had sent the cancellation email before the meeting ended.

It was a small victory for the process. It was also, Jayne thought, a small wound for Will. Being called out publicly by the newest member of the team was not the kind of moment a ten-year veteran processed easily.

Week five brought a harder test.

The technology modernization priority — the third of the three, owned by Olivia — was stalling. The vendor transition was more complex than anyone had estimated. Integration timelines had slipped. The systems analyst Alex had promised to reallocate was stuck on an operations project that turned out to be more urgent than expected.

Olivia brought it to the leadership meeting with the same precision she brought to everything: the timeline was behind by three weeks, the cost was running over by fifteen percent, and the root cause was resource contention between her priority and Alex's.

Alex, who had been professionally cordial but emotionally absent since the offsite, responded with something that was technically accurate and completely unhelpful: "The operations workstream is on track. I can't release the analyst without putting my milestones at risk."

Olivia looked at him. "Your milestones are a subset of our milestones. If the technology priority fails, it undermines both of us."

"Then we need more resources," Alex said. "Not a trade."

"We agreed to cut first and prove the model," Olivia said. "That was your father's call and the team aligned."

The mention of *your father* was subtle but it landed. Alex's face went flat again — the same expression from the offsite, the controlled blankness that Jayne recognized as his way of managing anger. Jayne was not typically in these meetings, but today James asked for her insight.

James stepped in. "Olivia's right. We committed to cutting first. But Alex is also right that we can't rob one priority to feed another." He paused. "Here's what I'm deciding: Alex, you keep the analyst for two more weeks to close out the critical path on your workstream. After that, they move to Olivia. And I'm going to find a budget within the existing plan to bridge the gap on the technology priority. It won't be the full amount. But it'll be enough to keep it moving."

"Fist to Five?" he said.

Threes and fours. Alex held up a three. It was the first time since the offside that his number had been above a two.

Progress. Not resolution. But progress.

Grace's backslide came in week six.

It happened in the Tuesday meeting — the same meeting where she'd been practicing restraint, where she'd been shorter, more deliberate, asking questions instead of narrating. She'd been doing well. Marcus had told Jayne he was cautioùsly optimistic.

The trigger was a discussion about a key hire for the client deepening initiative. Grace had sourced three candidates. Will had reviewed them and had concerns about all three. He raised them in the meeting — directly, as he'd been practicing — and Grace heard it as a rejection. Not of the candidates. Of her.

She launched into a defense. Not a monologue exactly, but the kind of extended, emotional response that the room had been hoping was behind them. She cited the brief she'd been given. She cited the timeline. She cited the three candidates' qualifications in detail. She referenced similar hires she'd made in 2019 and 2021 and how those had turned out well. She was hurt and she was showing it, and the more she talked the more the room contracted.

Will started to smooth. Then he stopped himself — visibly, physically stopped himself, his mouth closing on the bridging phrase he'd been about to offer.

James didn't redirect her this time. Jayne, who wasn't in the room but heard about it from three separate sources, thought that was probably wise. One public redirect was clarifying. Two would be humiliating.

It was Olivia who finally said, quietly, "Grace, I think Will is trying to help you find better candidates. Not reject your work."

Grace stopped. She looked at Olivia. She looked at Will. She looked at the table.

"You're right," she said. "I'm sorry. I heard that differently than it was intended."

She was quiet for the rest of the meeting. Not the intentional quiet of someone who was practicing restraint. The defeated quiet of someone who had just demonstrated, to herself and to everyone watching, that the old patterns were stronger than six weeks of coaching.

Marcus called Jayne that evening.

"She's going to want to quit," he said. "Not the company. The process. She's going to tell me next session that coaching isn't working and that maybe she's just not cut out for this team."

"What are you going to say?"

"I'm going to tell her that this is the work. That growth isn't a straight line. That what happened today wasn't a failure — it was a practice run, and the fact that she caught it and apologized in real time is something Grace from two months ago wouldn't have done."

"Will she hear that?"

"I don't know. But I'm going to say it anyway."

CHAPTER TWENTY

What James Sees Now

Jayne and James met in his office on a gray Wednesday afternoon, seven weeks after the offsite.

He looked tired. Not defeated — tired in the way of someone who had been carrying something heavy and was beginning to understand that carrying it was the job, not a temporary condition.

"How are you?" she asked.

"Honest answer?"

"Always."

"I thought it would be easier by now." He set his coffee down. "The offsite was — I don't know. Hard, but productive. I thought we'd come out of it and things would start clicking. And some things are. The operational efficiency work is ahead of schedule. The client deepening playbook is solid. But the technology priority is behind. Grace had a rough week. Alex is still cold with me. Someone restarted a project we killed, and I had to be the one to kill it again."

He looked at the window.

"I made the decisions. I held the line. I did everything we talked about. And it's not working the way I thought it would."

Jayne let the silence sit.

"What did you think it would look like?" she asked.

He almost laughed. "I thought everyone would see it. The clarity. The accountability. I thought if I just started being more decisive, the team would respond and everything would get better."

"And instead?"

"Instead, one of my priorities is stalling, my son barely talks to me outside of meetings, Grace is either overcorrecting or reverting, and I'm not sure Will has fully forgiven me for calling him out in front of the team." He paused. "I'm doing the right things. I think. And it's still messy."

"James," Jayne said. "This is what it looks like."

He looked at her.

"This is what real change looks like," she said. "It's messy. It's uneven. People don't transform in six weeks. Systems don't rewire overnight. You're not going to hit all three priorities perfectly. You might only hit two. Grace might take six more months to find her footing. Alex might not fully process the offsite until next year. Some of the stops might creep back. Some of the commitments might soften."

She leaned forward.

"But here's what's different. When the brand repositioning restarted, you caught it and you killed it. When Alex and Olivia were in a resource conflict, you made a call and the team aligned. When Grace backslid, the room handled it — not you alone, the room. Olivia named it. Grace heard it. She apologized in real time. That's not the same organization you were running three months ago."

"But the results—"

"The results are going to be imperfect," Jayne said. "They always are. You may or may not hit $195 million this year. You might not hit all three 90-day milestones. Some of this is going to take longer than you want."

She held his gaze.

"The question isn't whether the outcomes are perfect. The question is whether you have a process that works. A way of making decisions, holding each other accountable, and telling the truth — even when it's uncomfortable. You didn't have that three months ago. You have it now. It's not polished. It's not automatic. But it's real."

James was quiet for a long time.

"I called you to fix Grace," he said.

"You did."

"And what you actually fixed was the process."

"I didn't fix it," Jayne said. "You did. You and your team. I just held up the mirror."

He sat with that.

"The process is the fix," he said. Almost to himself. "Not the people. The process."

"The people are fine," Jayne said. "They always were. Imperfect, complicated, struggling in the ways that real leaders struggle. But fine. The thing that was broken was the system around them. The way decisions got made and unmade. The way accountability disappeared. The way hard conversations got avoided until they became crises."

She paused.

"You didn't have broken people, James. You had a broken process. And now you have the beginning of a better one."

He nodded. Not the reflexive nod she'd seen a hundred times. A slow, deliberate nod. The nod of someone who had finally arrived at the thing the whole engagement had been building toward.

"I want to have a conversation with Alex," he said. "A real one. Not about operations. About us. About what the COO role means and what succession looks like and how we work together without the father-son thing poisoning every interaction."

"That's a good conversation to have."

"And I want to talk to Grace. Tell her what I see — the progress and the backslide. All of it. Directly."

"That's a better conversation to have."

"And I need to thank Olivia. She's been the steadiest person on this team and I haven't told her that."

Jayne smiled.

"You've got a list," she said.

"I've got a list." He almost smiled back. "First time in a while the list has been about what *I* need to do, instead of what everyone else is doing wrong."

"That's the shift," Jayne said. "That's the whole thing."

CHAPTER TWENTY-ONE

The Moment of Truth

The test came nine weeks after the offsite, and it came in a form nobody expected.

Meridian's largest client — a health system that represented nearly twelve percent of total revenue — informed them that they were considering a competitive review of their contract. Not terminating. Reviewing. But in the language of client relationships, "competitive review" was one step from "goodbye."

The news hit the leadership team on a Monday morning. By Monday afternoon, James had called an emergency session.

In the old Meridian, this meeting would have gone a predictable way. James would have asked everyone what they thought. Will would have offered a diplomatic read. Grace would have pulled up the history. Alex would have proposed an operational response. Olivia would have run the numbers. And an hour later, they would have left without a clear decision about who was doing what by when.

That's not what happened.

James opened the meeting by stating the situation in two sentences. Then he said, "I'm going to tell you what I think we should do, and then I want to hear from each of you. But I'm making the call at the end of this meeting."

He proposed that he personally call the client CEO within forty-eight hours, accompanied by Will and Grace. Not to pitch. Not to defend. To listen.

Alex's instinct was different. He wanted to lead with a proposal — a revised service model, improved SLAs, a retention package.

Will said, "I think James's right. If we show up with a solution before we understand the problem, we're doing exactly what our 360 feedback says we do — moving fast without understanding what's actually needed."

Grace spoke next. She took a breath first — Jayne heard about it later, the visible pause, the conscious choice to be deliberate.

"I know this client. I've known them for eleven years. The relationship is real, but they've been frustrated with our responsiveness for the last eighteen months. I should have escalated that earlier, and I didn't." She paused. "Showing up to listen is the right move. And I think having me in the room matters because of the history. But I also think we need Alex's retention proposal ready as a follow-up within a week."

It was clear, specific, and honest about her own part in the problem. Not perfect — she'd talked a beat longer than she needed to. But the substance was there.

Olivia added the financial frame. "If we lose this client, the impact is significant. But the cost of a bad retention deal is worse. Listening first is right."

James looked around the room. "Fist to Five."

Three fives. One four. One three.

Alex was the three. "I'll align," he said. "And I'll have the retention proposal ready for the follow-up."

It wasn't enthusiasm. But it was real, and the room knew the difference between Alex's three today and his two at the offsite. Something had shifted, even if it hadn't fully resolved.

They went to the client. They listened. What they heard wasn't what they expected.

The client's frustration wasn't primarily about service quality. It was about feeling like Meridian had stopped paying attention — that the company had grown and the client had become just another account instead of a partnership. It was, Jayne realized when James told her about it later, the organizational version of the same problem James had with Grace: not a broken relationship, but a neglected one.

Alex's retention proposal, when it came, was good. The client agreed to stay, with conditions. It was a save, but not a clean one — Meridian had to invest in a dedicated account team and restructure the service agreement. It costs money. It cost time. And it wouldn't have been necessary if someone had been paying attention eighteen months earlier.

Grace knew that. She said it in the debrief, plainly, without defensiveness: "This was partly on me. I saw the warning signs and I didn't flag them. That's going to change."

It was the kind of accountability that the old system had never required of her. The new one did.

CHAPTER TWENTY-TWO

Jayne Reflects

I don't usually let myself get attached to outcomes.

It's one of the first things I learned in this work — that the coach's job is to hold the space, not to need the result. You show up. You ask the questions. You create the conditions for change. And then you let people choose.

Sometimes they choose well. Sometimes they don't. Sometimes they choose well for six weeks and then revert so completely that you wonder if the whole engagement was theater.

I've seen all of it.

Meridian didn't give me a clean ending. That's what makes it real.

The offsite wasn't perfect. Alex walked out. Grace had a rough moment and then a worse one three weeks later. The stop list partially unraveled within a month. The technology priority fell behind schedule and stayed behind. Of the three priorities, only operational efficiency was fully on track at the ninety-day mark. Revenue was progressing but uneven. Technology was struggling.

Grace was better. Not "fixed" — better. She was shorter in meetings. She asked more questions. She caught herself more often. She also backslid, and when she did, it was painful for everyone in the room. Marcus told me she would be a different leader in a year. He wasn't sure she'd be a different leader in three months. Neither was I.

Alex was still carrying the offsite. The walkout. The geographic expansion being killed. The moment his father chose the company's direction over his recommendation. He was performing alignment, and the performance was getting better, but it wasn't the same as the real thing. Dina said he needed a conversation with James that went deeper than strategy — a conversation about family, about trust, about what it means to be both a son and a successor. That conversation hadn't happened yet. It might not happen during this engagement. Some things take their own time.

Will was finding his voice. Slowly, imperfectly, with frequent retreats into the diplomacy that had kept him safe for a decade. But there were moments — small, genuine moments — where he said what he actually thought instead of what the room wanted to hear. Tom told me those moments were becoming more frequent. That was enough.

Olivia had become the team's anchor. Steady, precise, increasingly willing to name what others wouldn't. She was the one who caught the brand repositioning restart. She was the one who pushed Alex on the resource conflict. She was also, I suspected, going to play an increasingly important role in whatever this company became next.

What got to me was James.

Not the offsite James, though that was meaningful. Instead the James sat in his office seven weeks later and said that he'd been doing everything right and it was still messy. The James who had expected clarity to produce results and was learning that clarity produces something harder and more important: it produces the truth. About where you are, what's working, what isn't, and what the gap between your aspirations and your reality actually looks like.

He didn't hit all three priorities. He wasn't going to. The company may or may not reach $195 million this year. The technology modernization was behind, and realistically, it was going to stay behind until the capital-ask went through.

But here's what changed: when the brand repositioning restarted, someone caught it. When the technology priority stalled, the team had a process for resolving the resource conflict. When the biggest client threatened to leave, five people sat in a room, made a decision in thirty minutes, and executed. When Grace backslid, the room handled it — not with silence, not with James's old avoidance, but with honesty.

The outcomes were imperfect. The process was working.

That's the thing I try to help every CEO I work with understand. The fix is never the person you called me about. And the fix isn't the offsite, or the 360, or the coaching, or the framework on the flip chart. Those are tools. They're useful. But they're not the fix.

The fix is the process. The way decisions get made and held. The way people talk to each other when it's uncomfortable. The way accountability shows up not as punishment but as a shared commitment to doing what you said you'd do. The way a leader looks at the system instead of the symptom.

James called me to fix Grace.

What he found was that Grace didn't need fixing. She needed a system that worked. She needed expectations she could see and standards she could measure herself against and a leader who was willing to tell her the truth directly, kindly, and without waiting until it became a crisis.

She needed what every person on that team needed.

Not better people. A better process.

I'm not naïve about what comes next. The coaching engagements will continue through the quarter. Some milestones will be met. Some won't. There will be setbacks and arguments and weeks when every person in that room wonders if the offsite changed anything at all.

But the system is different now. The person at the top got honest about his own role in it. He stopped looking outward for the problem and started looking at himself. And in doing that, he gave everyone else permission to do the same.

That's not a resolution. It's a beginning.

But in twenty years of doing this work, I've learned that the beginning is the part that matters most. Because the hardest thing isn't changing behavior. The hardest thing is building a process that can hold the truth — even when the truth is that you're behind schedule, that your team is still struggling, that the person you wanted to blame is actually the person who needed your clarity most.

The wrong fix is the one that starts with someone else.

The right fix is the process that starts with you.

EPILOGUE

Six Months Later

James Wilson left the house at seven-fifteen on a Monday morning.

Same coffee shop. Same medium dark roast. Same eight-minute drive to the office.

The silence in the car was different, though. Not empty. Not anxious. More like the silence between movements in a piece of music — a rest that was part of the composition, not a gap in it.

He had a full day ahead. A leadership team meeting at nine — shorter now, tighter, with an agenda that actually ended when it was supposed to. A call with the health system client at eleven — the relationship was rebuilding, not rebuilt, and it was going to take another quarter of consistent attention before the trust was fully back. An afternoon session with his new VP of Technology, a hire that Grace had sourced and Olivia had vetted and the whole team had agreed on in a single meeting.

He'd spoken with Jayne last week. The formal coaching engagement was winding down. The team still had work to do — it would always have work to do — but the work was different now. It was maintenance, not construction. The foundation had been poured. Some of the walls were still going up.

He still had problems. The company still had friction. Revenue was tracking closer to plan but not perfectly — they were going to finish the year around $185 million, short of the original $195 million target but well ahead of where they'd been trending before the offsite. The technology modernization was behind schedule. It was going to be a two-quarter initiative instead of one, and James had learned to be honest about that instead of pretending the original timeline was still alive.

The geographic expansion was back on the table. Alex had brought a revised expansion proposal at the end of Q1, as promised, with data and a clear execution plan. James had decided they would hold off on starting that until the beginning of Q3, so approved but with conditions. It was happening — but on terms that the team had agreed to, not on the terms Alex had originally wanted. He was learning to live with that. Some days are better than others.

They'd had the conversation. The real one — about the COO role, about succession, about being father and son in the same company. It hadn't fixed everything. It had opened a door that had been closed, and now they were both standing in the doorway, figuring out what the room looked like. Dina said it would take a year. James believed her.

Grace was still Grace. She still talked a beat too long sometimes. She still carried the binder. But she was different in ways that mattered — faster, more precise, more willing to ask a question before offering an answer. She had hard weeks. She had weeks where Marcus had to remind her that growth wasn't a straight line. But her team was performing. The talent pipeline was moving. And the honest conversation James had with her — the one he should have had two years ago — had changed something between them. Not the warmth, which had always been there. The clarity, which hadn't.

Will had surprised everyone, including himself. In a leadership meeting two months after the offsite, he'd openly disagreed with James about a client strategy — not diplomatically, not through a reframe, but directly. "I think you're wrong about this, and here's why." James had listened, pushed back, and ultimately changed his mind. Afterward, Will had sent Tom a two-word text: *That worked.*

Olivia had become the team's anchor. She'd presented the Q2 results to the full leadership team — at James's suggestion — and the feedback afterward was consistent: not praise for the numbers, which were mixed, but praise for the clarity and the honesty about what wasn't working.

Transparent. Not perfect. Transparent.

James had started to understand that those were not the same thing, and that the second was worth more than the first.

He turned into the parking garage and found his spot.

He sat for a moment with the engine running.

He thought about where he'd been six months ago — sitting in this same spot, frustrated, convinced that Grace was the problem, ready to call someone to fix her. He thought about the podcast that had caught him mid-commute, and the woman on it who had described his company without knowing it existed.

He thought about the question she'd asked. The one about the last decision he'd made that was successfully executed.

He had a list of those now. Some had been right. Some hadn't. The technology timeline had been too aggressive — he'd known it in his gut at the offsite and had committed to it anyway. The decision to stop the geographic expansion had been right at the time, even though it had cost him something with Alex that was still being repaid.

Not all the decisions were good. But they were *his*. They were clear. And the team had a process for making them, challenging them, and living with them.

That, he was beginning to understand, was the whole point.

He turned off the engine. Picked up his phone. Opened his podcast app.

A new episode had dropped overnight. He didn't recognize the guest, but the title caught his eye: *Built to Execute: Where the Work Actually Happens.*

He smiled.

He put in his earbuds and started walking.

He had eight minutes before the day started.

AFTERWORD

A Note from the Author

Jayne Swan is not a real person. James Wilson, Grace Matthews, Alex, Will, and Olivia are not real people. Meridian doesn't exist.

But this story is true.

Before I founded Cross Impact in 2014, I spent years leading large-scale technology transformations: $100M+ programs across healthcare, finance, insurance, and technology. I was brought in to execute. But over and over, senior leaders would pull me aside not to talk about the technology, but about the people responsible for leading it. The misalignment. The politics. The decisions that weren't getting made.

That pattern, repeated across industries, company sizes, and leadership styles, is what led me to do the work I do today. And it's the pattern at the heart of this book.

The CEO who calls me about one person on his team. I've had that conversation dozens of times. The name changes. The title changes. Sometimes it's the CFO who can't communicate without putting people on the defensive. Sometimes it's the COO who is great with systems but terrible with people. Sometimes it really is the head of HR. And the CEO is always patient when he or she describes it. They always want me to know that they've tried.

And almost every time, after I listen and take notes and ask a few questions, I start to see the same thing James saw in this story: the person they're calling about is a symptom. The problem lives somewhere else.

No two engagements look the same. Some start with a struggling leadership team that has never learned to make a decision and commit to it. Some start with a founder who has outgrown his own management style but doesn't have language for it yet. Some start with a succession crisis, or a merger that exposed fault lines nobody had mapped, or a board that has stopped trusting the CEO and a CEO who doesn't fully understand why. Some take ninety days. Some take two years. Some are resolved in a single offsite that changes the trajectory of an organization. Some require patient, unglamorous work that doesn't show results until the second or third quarter.

But the outcome tends in the same direction. And it tends that way for a reason I've come to believe deeply after more than a decade of this work:

When you fix the system, the people can do their jobs.

That's not a soft idea. It's not a reframe designed to let struggling leaders off the hook. It's what I've seen again and again, in companies across healthcare, insurance, technology, financial services, retail and beyond. The leaders I work with are not broken. They are often genuinely talented, deeply committed, and working hard. What they're missing is what I've come to call a Leadership Operating System: the shared behaviors, decision frameworks, and execution rhythms that turn a group of strong individuals into a team that operates as one.

Most leadership teams have the talent. What they're missing is alignment. And alignment isn't a personality trait. It's a system. It can be built. It can be taught. And when it's in place, the things that looked like people problems often resolve on their own.

I've watched COOs who were labeled as "not strategic enough" become genuine organizational leaders once someone gave them a clear mandate and held the line on expectations. I've watched HR executives who were written off as out of touch become indispensable partners once they had real feedback and a leader willing to be direct. I've watched CEOs who had been circling the same unresolved tensions for years finally move forward once they stopped asking for consensus and started making calls.

None of those transformations were clean. None of them happened in a single offsite or a single feedback session or a single honest conversation, though all of those things mattered. Real change is messy and uneven and slower than everyone wants it to be. There are setbacks. There are weeks when the old patterns reassert themselves with the quiet force of a tide coming in. There are moments when the leader you're working with has to choose, again, between the easy path and the right one.

But the outcomes are real. I know this because my clients tell me, not just at the end of an engagement, but months and years later. They tell me about the hard conversation they finally had. About the decision they made and held. About the team member who found their footing once the expectations became clear. About the year their company stopped spinning and started moving.

If you picked up this book because you recognized something in the opening pages: the CEO on the phone, the person he's calling about, the quiet conviction that if you could just fix that one person, everything else would fall into place. I wrote it for you.

Not to tell you that you're the problem. But to ask you to look somewhere you may not have looked yet.

The system is always worth examining. And in my experience, the leaders who are willing to examine it, honestly, with the same rigor they'd apply to a financial audit or an operational review, are the ones whose teams eventually become the kind of teams that other leaders envy.

Not because those leaders were the most talented. But because they were willing to start with themselves.

Betsy Kauffman
Founder & CEO, Cross Impact
crossimpact.co

www.ingramcontent.com/pod-product-compliance
Lightning Source LLC
LaVergne TN
LVHW051005080826
845145LV00009B/2475